The Reign Of Antoninus Pius

Ernest Edward Bryant

In the interest of creating a more extensive selection of rare historical book reprints, we have chosen to reproduce this title even though it may possibly have occasional imperfections such as missing and blurred pages, missing text, poor pictures, markings, dark backgrounds and other reproduction issues beyond our control. Because this work is culturally important, we have made it available as a part of our commitment to protecting, preserving and promoting the world's literature. Thank you for your understanding.

Cambridge Historical Essays. No. VIII.

THE

REIGN OF ANTONINUS PIUS

BY

E. E. BRYANT, B.A.

FELLOW OF EMMANUEL COLLEGE, CAMBRIDGE.

THIRLWALL DISSERTATION, 1894.

Cambridge:
AT THE UNIVERSITY PRESS.
1895

[*All Rights reserved.*]

PREFACE.

It is a noteworthy fact that hitherto no attempt has been made to produce an exhaustive chronological sketch of the reign of Antoninus Pius. Merivale[1] seems to have given up all idea either of arranging the events of this reign in chronological sequence or of including any detailed information in his work. Schiller[2] devotes a few pages to the juxtaposition of details without any attempt at arrangement or pretence to exhaustive treatment; while Lacour-Gayet[3] has composed an interminable series of essays on various phases of the life and times of Antoninus Pius, building up his theories on very slender foundations and not attempting to give a chronological sketch of the whole reign.

[1] Merivale. *History of the Roman Empire.*
[2] Schiller. *Geschichte der römischen Kaiserzeit.*
[3] Lacour-Gayet. *Antonin le Pieux et son temps.*

This essay, which by permission of the examiners for the Thirlwall Prize has been corrected in a few places before being printed, aims at giving a chronological sketch of Antoninus Pius's reign together with a discussion of the relations of the Emperor with various individuals and bodies in the Roman state. His relations with religious bodies I have discussed at considerable length and I fear that the chapter dealing with this point may be out of proportion to the rest of the essay. But it seemed to me impossible to clearly state Pius's position with regard to Christianity without first giving a fairly exhaustive sketch of the circumstances which led up to that position.

I have placed at the commencement of my essay a list of the books to which reference has been made in the following pages, and of the abbreviations which I have used. In neither case is the list quite complete; but I have referred only incidentally to those books which I have not included in the list, while the abbreviations not included will explain themselves readily.

Among the modern writers to whom I am more especially indebted may be mentioned *Eckhel* and *Cohen* for their most valuable works on the coins of the period; *Waddington* for his discussion of exact dates connected with the life of Aristides; *Willems* and in a less degree *Madvig* and *Mommsen* for their information on constitutional points; and *Ramsay*, *Hardy* and *Wiltsch* for their writings on the position and extent of Christianity under the Roman Emperors.

My thanks are due to Mr P. Giles of this college, who has most kindly undertaken the labour of correcting the proofs of this essay. I am also indebted to him for the many valuable suggestions with which he has from time to time assisted me.

E. E. BRYANT.

EMMANUEL COLLEGE, CAMBRIDGE.
August 8, 1895.

BOOKS TO WHICH REFERENCE IS MADE.

ABBREVIATIONS.

C. I. L.	Corpus inscriptionum Latinarum (Berlin, 1863–).
C. I. G.	,, ,, Graecarum (Berlin, 1828–1877).
C. I. A.	,, ,, Atticarum (Berlin, 1873–).
C. I. Rh.	,, ,, Rhenanarum (1867).
Inscr. Gr. Sept.	,, ,, Graecarum Graeciae Septentrionalis (Berlin, 1892).
Inscr. Gr. Sic. et Ital.	Inscriptiones Graecae Siciliae et Italiae (Berlin, 1890).
Letronne, *Inscr. Egypt.*	Letronne. Latin and Greek inscriptions of Egypt (Paris, 1842–1848).
Wilmanns	Wilmanns. Selected inscriptions (Berlin, 1873).
Orelli	Orelli. Selected Latin inscriptions (Zürich, 1828–1856).
Marm. Grut.	Gruter. Inscriptiones Romanae (1616).
Inscr. de l'Asie Min.	Le Bas et Waddington. Greek inscriptions of Greece and Asia Minor (Paris, 1848–1870).
Henzen	Henzen. Inscriptiones Urbis Romae Latinae (Berlin, 1876).
de Rossi, *Rom. Sott.*	de Rossi. Roma Sotteranea (London, 1879).
Mon. Anc.	Monumentum Ancyranum (Mommsen. Berlin, 1883).
Eph. Ep.	Ephemeris Epigraphica (Rome, 1872–).
Eckhel	Eckhel. Doctrina Nummorum Veterum (Vienna, 1792–1798).
Cohen *or* Cohen, *Ant. P.*	Cohen. Les Monnaies frappées sous l'empire romain. (Vol. ii., Reign of Antoninus Pius.) (Paris, 1882.)
	Mommsen. (Blacas.) Histoire de la Monnaie romaine. (Paris, 1873).
V. Hadr., V. Hel., V. P., V. M., V. Ver., V. Avid. Cass., V. Alex. Sev.	Scriptores Historiae Augustae (Teubner, 1884): Vitae Hadriani, Helii, Antonini Pii, Marci Antonini Veri, Avidii Cassii, Alexandri Severi.

BOOKS TO WHICH REFERENCE IS MADE.

ABBREVIATIONS
M. Aur. εἰς ἑαυτ.   M. Aurelius. εἰς ἑαυτόν (Teubner).
Arist.   Aristides (Dindorf. Leipzig, 1829).
Paus.   Pausanias (Bekker. Berlin, 1826, 1827).
                       Arrian. Periplus (Hoffmann. Leipzig, 1842).
App. *Proem.*, *B.C.* } Appian. Proemium *and* Bellum Civile (Teubner).
 or 'Εμφ.   }
Dio C.   Dio Cassius (Teubner).
Xiph. *or* Xiph. *D.C.* Xiphilinus   ,,
Zon.   Zonaras   ,,
Eutr.   Eutropius   ,,
Aur. Vict.   S. Aurelius Victor. De Caesaribus.
Plin. *Epp.*   C. Plinius Secundus (Keil. Leipzig, 1870).
Pliny-Trajan   ,,   ,,   Correspondence with Trajan (E. G. Hardy. London, 1889).
Plin. *H. N.*   ,,   ,,   (maior). Historia Naturalis (Teubner).
M. Corn. Front.   M. Cornelius Fronto (Berlin, 1816).
Oros.   Orosius (Teubner).
                       Malala (Dindorf. Bonn, 1831).
Val. Max.   Valerius Maximus (Teubner).
                       Strabo (Teubner).
Vell.   Velleius Paterculus (Teubner).
                       Suidas (Gaisford. Oxford, 1834).
                       Festus (Budapesth, 1889).
Philostr. *V. Soph.*   Philostratus. Vita Sophistarum (Kayser. Zürich, 1844).
                       Lucian (Teubner).
Apul. *Apol.*, *Flor.* Apuleius. Apology *and* Florida (Hildebrand. Leipzig, 1842).
Gell. *Noct. Att.*   Aulus Gellius. Noctes Atticae (Teubner).
Tac. *Ann.*, *Agr.*   Tacitus. Annals *and* Agricola   ,,
Suet.   Suetonius. De vita Caesarum   ,,
Euseb. *H. E.*   Eusebius. Historia Ecclesiastica   ,,
Just.   Justin Martyr (Otto. Jena, 1876).
Clement. *Str.*, *ad Marc.* Clement. Stromateis *and* ad Marcionem (Migne's Patrology. Paris, 1857).
Sulp. Sev.   Sulpicius Severus (Migne's Patrology. Paris, 1857).
Anacl.   Anacletus   ,,   ,,
                       Soter   ,,   ,,
Anic.   Anicetus   ,,   ,,

BOOKS TO WHICH REFERENCE IS MADE.

ABBREVIATIONS.
Acts   Acts of the Apostles.
Tert.   Tertullian (Bindley. Oxford, 1889–1893).
                  Apology of Aristides (Texts and Studies. Cambridge, 1891).
Orig. c. Cels.   Origen. Contra Celsum (Cambridge, 1876).
                  Polycarp (Lightfoot. London, 1885).
Joseph.   Josephus (Dindorf. Paris, 1845–1847).
Just. Inst.   Justinian. Institutiones (Sandars. London, 1888).
                  Gaius (Studemund. Berlin, 1884).

Schiller, *Geschichte*   Schiller. Geschichte der römischen Kaiserzeit (Gotha, 1883).
Lacour-Gayet, *Ant. P.*   Lacour-Gayet. Antonin le Pieux et son temps (Paris, 1888).
J. J. Müller   J. J. Müller (Büdinger's Untersuchungen zur römischen Kaisergeschichte. Leipzig, 1871–).
                  Schurz. De Mutationibus in Imperio Romano ordinando ab Imperatore Hadriano factis (Bonn, 1883).
Wadd. *Mém.*   Waddington. Mémoires sur la vie du rhéteur Aristide (Mém. de l'Acad., 1867).
Wadd. *Fast. Asiat.*   „   Fasti Asiatici.
                  Klein. Fasti Consulares (Leipzig, 1881).
                  Borghesi. Œuvres (Paris, 1862).
                  Cagnat. L'Armée romaine d'Afrique (1892).
Willems, *D. P. R.*   Willems. Le droit public romain (Paris, 1888).
Madv. *Röm. Staat.*   Madvig. Die Verfassung und Verwaltung des römischen Staates (Leipzig, 1881).
Momms.   Mommsen. Staatsrecht (Leipzig, 1871–).
                  Roby. Introduction to the Study of the Digest (Cambridge, 1884).
Ramsay   Ramsay. The Church in the Roman Empire (London, 1893).
Hardy   Hardy. Christianity and the Roman Government (London, 1894).
                  Lightfoot. Apostolic Fathers (London, 1885).
                  G. Boissier. La religion romaine d'Auguste aux Antonins (Paris, 1874).
                  Friedländer. Darstellungen aus der Sittengeschichte Roms (Leipzig, 1888–1890).

ABBREVIATIONS.

Wiltsch   Wiltsch. Handbook of the Geography and Statistics of the Church (translated by J. Leitch. 1859–1868).

Le Quien. Œuvres (Paris, 1712).

Ruinart. Acta Martyrum (Amsterdam, 1713).

ABBREVIATIONS OTHER THAN THOSE USED FOR REFERENCE.

Aed. Div. Aug. Rest.	= Aedis Divi Augusti Restituta.
Cos.	= Consul.
Cos. Des.	= Consul designatus.
D. d.	= Dono dedit.
Imp. Caes. Aug.	= Imperator Caesar Augustus.
K. Febr.	= Kalendae Februariae.
Leg.	= Legio.
Leg. X. g. p. f.	= Legio X. gemina, pia fidelis.
Leg. I. adiutr.	= Legio I. adiutrix.
Leg. Aug. pr. pr. prov.	= Legatus Augusti pro praetore provinciae.
Leg. leg.	= Legatus Legionis.
Lib.	= Liberalitas.
M. F.	= Marci filius.
Pii F.	= Pii filius.
P. P.	= Pater patriae.
P. M.	= Pontifex Maximus.
Praef. Praet.	= Praefectus Praetorio.
Praef. urbi	= Praefectus urbi.
Pr. Eq.	= Praefectus equitibus.
Pr.	= Praetor.
Pr. C. R.	= Praetor civium Romanorum.
Proc.	= Procurator.
Procos.	= Proconsul.
Procos. Imp.	= Proconsulare Imperium.

ABBREVIATIONS.

Quaest.	= Quaestor.
S. C.	= Senatus consultum.
S. P. Q. R.	= Senatus Populusque Romanus.
Trib. Mil.	= Tribunus Militum.
Tr. pl.	= Tribunus plebis.
Tr. P. Tr. Pot. Trib. Pot.	= Tribunicia potestas.
Vot.	= Vota.
Vota Sol. Dec.	= Vota soluta Decennalia.

ERRATA.

P. 42, n. 4, *for* Appuleius *read* Apuleius.

P. 59, line 12, *for* (Lib. III.) *read* (Lib. IV.).

P. 83, n. 5 and p. 85, n. 3, *for* Henzen, 5430 *read* Henzen, 5480.

CONTENTS.

		PAGE
Preface		v
Books to which Reference is made		ix
Abbreviations		xiii
Chapter I.	Authorities	1
Chapter II.	The early life of Antoninus	7
Chapter III.	Reign of Antoninus Pius till 148 A.D.	25
Chapter IV.	Reign of Antoninus Pius, 148—161 A.D.	65
Chapter V.	The Emperor and the Empire	93
	§ 1. Personal details and character	93
	§ 2. M. Aurelius and L. Verus	98
	§ 3. The Senate	103
	§ 4. The Consilium Principis	108
	§ 5. Italy	115
	§ 6. The Provinces	122
	§ 7. Men of Letters	130
Chapter VI.	Religion	141
Index		207

THE REIGN OF ANTONINUS PIUS.

CHAPTER I.

AUTHORITIES.

IN order to give anything approaching to a clear view of the history of the reign of Antoninus Pius it is necessary to gather together information from the most varied sources. Those ancient historians, who set before themselves the task of giving a sketch of his reign and whose works have been preserved to us, were either incapable of estimating critically the relative importance of the events which they wished to describe, or were unwilling to undertake the task of presenting anything beyond an ill-arranged assortment of unconnected details; they lived too for the most part at a considerable distance from the times of which they were writing, and were thus dependent on the information supplied by contemporary writers and on the oral traditions which existed. But beyond all this the reign of Antoninus Pius was devoid of events of great political importance and, while it is a period full of interest to the critical student, contains little to arrest the attention of the average writer. The contemporary writers deal for the most part with the manners and customs and the intellectual life of the period, and it is left to secondary authorities to piece together a political history of the times; but their efforts are poor, and it needs some investigation before we can gather from their works anything beyond the general idea that the Roman Empire flourished under Antoninus Pius.

Of contemporary writers *M. Aurelius* in his Meditations gives little or no information concerning political events, but is invaluable for the testimony which he gives as to the life at the Imperial Court and the character of Antoninus both as a man and as an Emperor. *Lucian, Apuleius* and *Aulus Gellius* reflect the literary thought and the manners of their times and incidentally throw some light on the condition of the provinces. *M. Cornelius Fronto* was a man of considerable importance in the reigns of Antoninus Pius and M. Aurelius and held the position of tutor to the latter. Many letters which passed between him and Antoninus Pius or M. Aurelius are preserved. They deal for the most part with literary or purely domestic affairs but also contain references to matters of greater moment such as the relations existing between Pius and Marcus. *Aristides*, a prolific writer of the period, composed a number of orations which are still extant; they deal in some cases with the condition of the provinces under the Empire and especially in the reign of Pius, and contain general statements as to the nature of Antoninus Pius's rule. Aristides is a writer who must be carefully consulted for this period, but it must be remembered that he is amazingly prone to exaggerated and absurd statements. *Pausanias* gives considerable information concerning the buildings erected in Greece by Pius, while *Arrian* and *Appian* may be consulted with advantage for the history of the provinces. A writer of a different stamp is *Justin Martyr*, whose writings may in part be placed within this reign. His Apologies and the Dialogue with Trypho are the most useful of his works for our period; they show the condition of the Christians in the reign of Antoninus Pius, and are clear contradictions of later writers who wished to show Pius in the light of a great friend to the Christians[1]. But it is from *Coins* and *Inscriptions* that by far the most important part of the contemporary information comes, and in the absence of all systematic contemporary " History " too great importance cannot be attached to these sources of knowledge. In fact, for determining the date of any event in this reign it is often necessary to rely solely on coins, and from them alone a sketch of the reign might be pieced together, which would be both more complete and more correct than the accounts given by many writers. Inscriptions too give great assistance in determining dates, while for any exact details of the period they supply perhaps the only trustworthy information.

It is with the secondary authorities that the systematic Histories of the reign of Antoninus Pius begin. Foremost among these come the Lives of the Roman

[1] I have not thought it worth while to make separate reference to the *Apology of Aristides*, which is of little value for historical purposes.

Emperors in the *Scriptores Historiae Augustae*; *Julius Capitolinus* on the Lives of Antoninus Pius, M. Antoninus Philosophus and Verus, *Aelius Spartianus* on Hadrian and Helius, and *Vulcacius Gallicanus* on Avidius Cassius wrote their narratives in the reigns of Diocletian and Constantine, some 150 years after the events which they describe. Their works can scarcely be described as Histories; they are rather collections of interesting scraps of information, composed in a bad literary style and with no regard to chronological sequence or historical accuracy; they cannot be used by themselves to determine any point exactly, but they appear for the most part to be fairly trustworthy, as far as they go. They are based almost entirely[1] on the works of *Marius Maximus*, whose writings are lost, and contain many quotations[2] from that writer, while they state many facts with the prefix[3] of "fertur" or "dicitur," which seem to be sure evidences of borrowing. This Marius Maximus[4] lived from about 162 A.D. to 234 A.D. and held the highest offices of state, including the proconsulship of Africa; his works seem to have been fairly widely read[5], since they satisfied the taste for gossip and scrappy information which characterized the times. Besides the Scriptores Historiae Augustae, *Eutropius*, who lived in the time of Constantine, wrote an Epitome of Roman History in 10 books; his work is good so far as it goes and is based on sound authorities, but it is not a

---

[1] Cf. J. J. Müller in Büdinger's *Untersuchungen zur Römischen Kaisergeschichte*, Vol. iii. pp. 19—200.
[2] *V. P.* 11, 3, and cf. Müller, p. 43.   [3] Cf. Müller, p. 45.
[4] Cf. Müller, pp. 171—173.   [5] Cf. Müller, p. 169.

critical or exhaustive history and aims only at conveying a little information in a pleasing manner with very little discrimination as to what is politically important. *Eusebius*, living from 264 to 340 A.D., wrote an Ecclesiastical History based on the Church records and on the works of the Apologists and Fathers; he is our principal authority after Justin Martyr for the condition of the Christians at this period, but he himself says[1] that he suppresses everything that is to the discredit of the Christians. *Philostratus* wrote Βίοι Σοφιστῶν about the year 230 A.D. and in this work are included the lives of many literary men of the time of Antoninus Pius; his writing is rather of the interesting than of the accurate type and deals principally with matters of no political importance, though occasional references are made to political events. *S. Aurelius Victor* (circ. 350 A.D.) in his work "De Caesaribus" and his Epitome gives some very brief references to our period, but his work is practically valueless and seems to be based on nothing more sound than oral tradition. *Orosius* was a Spaniard living in the reign of Honorius who wrote a History of Rome to show that the calamities of his time were not due to the fact that Rome had cast aside her heathen gods; he bases his history for our period on Eutropius and Eusebius, but is of little assistance. *Malala* (circ. 580 A.D.) gives a certain amount of information not preserved elsewhere, but it is doubtful how far his statements can be accepted when uncorroborated by other evidence. One of the most serious losses which we have to deplore in compiling a history of this reign, is the loss of the works

[1] Euseb. *H. E.* viii. 2.

of Dio Cassius, whether in their original form or in their abridgement by *Xiphilinus* and *Zonaras*. These two epitomists, who are careless and faulty at the best of times, abridged the works of Dio Cassius about 1100 A.D. and in their writings several books of Dio Cassius are preserved, which are lost in their original form. Unfortunately the work of Dio Cassius on the reign of Antoninus Pius was already[1] lost before 1100 A.D. and the epitomists had therefore to fall back on other and inferior sources; the result is that their accounts of the reign of Antoninus Pius are comparatively worthless and contain scarcely one fact which is not better related elsewhere.

Such—with the addition of a brief notice in *Suidas*—is the stock of information at our disposal. It is a considerable stock, but contains—at least in the works of professed historians—nothing which can be considered as first-class information on political events. Manners, customs etc. may be fairly clearly seen in the works of various contemporary writers; but there is no great historian, contemporary or otherwise, to whom reference for this period can be made. It is more than ever essential to fall back upon inscriptions and coins; they are most useful for the history of any period, but for such a period as the reign of Antoninus Pius, which had no historian of merit to celebrate its course, they are absolutely invaluable.

[1] Xiph. 70. 1, 1.

CHAPTER II.

THE EARLY LIFE OF ANTONINUS.

ON September 19th, 86 A.D.[1], when the Emperor Domitian was consul for the 12th time and Cornelius Dolabella for the 1st time, there was born at a country house near Lanuvium a child who was destined to become Emperor fifty-two years afterwards. His name according to Capitolinus[2] was Titus Aurelius Fulvus Boionius Antoninus; Eutropius[3] calls him Fulvius, but an inscription[4] shows that Fulvus is the correct form of the name. The same inscription adds to him the name of Arrius which is found also in Capitolinus[5]. On the father's side[6] the family of T. Aurelius Fulvus Boionius Arrius Antoninus came originally from the town of Nemausus in Gallia Narbonensis,—a town of considerable size and importance lying in the fertile and well-watered district to the west of the mouth of

[1] *V. P.* 1, 8.   [2] *V. P.* 1, 1.   [3] Eutrop. viii. 8.
[4] *C. I. L.* viii. 8239.   [5] *V. P.* 4, 2.
[6] *Genealogical Table of Antoninus*, *V. P.* 1, 1—7.

```
        T. Aurelius Fulvus    Arrius Antoninus = Boionia Priscilla
               |                        |
         Aurelius Fulvus   =   Arria Fadilla — Julius Lupus
                                 |
             Antoninus Pius = Annia Faustina   Julia Fadilla
   ┌──────────────────┬──────────────────┬──────────────────┬──────────────────┐
   M. Aurelius Fulvus   M. Galerius Aur.   Aurelia Fadilla    Galeria Faustina
      Antoninus            Antoninus       = Lamia Silanus   = M. Aur. Antoninus
    C. I. L. vi. 988.    C. I. L. vi. 989.  C. I. vi. L. 990.   Eutrop. viii. 8.
```

the Rhone, at a distance of 20 miles from the coast and about 14 miles from the bank of the river, and situated on the Via Domitia, the high road which extended from the north of Italy along the south coast of Gaul into Spain. The town was accordingly in a most advantageous position for trade and formed a commercial centre for communication between the valley of the Rhone, Spain and the north of Italy. It is then a reasonable conjecture that the ancestors of Antoninus became wealthy through trade at Nemausus before they followed the example of so many rich provincial families and migrated to Rome, a conjecture which is supported by the fact that one of the first actions of Antoninus, when he had become Emperor, was to improve the means of communication[1] and to restore the roads of Gallia Narbonensis in the interests of commerce, as though he were paying back to that district some of the advantages which his family had received therefrom.

The first member of the family who is known to have held office at Rome was[2] Antoninus Pius's father's father, T. Aurelius Fulvus, who after holding various offices became consul for the second time and subsequently *praefectus urbis*. Antoninus's father[3] was Aurelius Fulvus, "homo tristis et integer," who once held the consulship. He probably died comparatively young, since his wife[4] married twice, while Antoninus was educated[5] by his grandfathers. On his mother's side Antoninus had for grandfather[6] Arrius Antoninus, who held the consulship twice, "homo sanctus et qui Nervam

---

[1] *C. I. L.* xii. viae publicae.   [2] *V. P.* 1, 2.   [3] *V. P.* 1, 3.
[4] *V. P.* 1, 5 and 6.   [5] *V. P.* 1, 9.   [6] *V. P.* 1, 4.

miseratus esset, quod imperare coepisset," while his mother Arria Fadilla married[1] twice, first Aurelius Fulvus and second Julius Lupus, a man of consular rank to whom she bore a daughter Julia Fadilla.

The child who was subsequently to become the governor of the Roman Empire came of a good family which though provincial in origin had already had many years, and at least three generations, in which to become adapted to the life of Rome—a family, which in its various branches had held some of the most dignified and important offices of state. Trajan, who came from Spain, was more distinctly provincial than Antoninus[2], yet the latter carried on the policy of true friendship[3] to the provinces, which had been one of the marked characteristics of the two preceding reigns, and in particular, the province which had been the cradle of his family profited by his accession. Eutropius[4] says he was "genere claro sed non admodum vetere," which corresponds exactly with the facts that are known concerning his origin.

Born at Lanuvium in 86 A.D. he spent his early years at Lorium[5] in a villa belonging to the Aurelii. Lorium he seems always to have regarded as his home, for he built a palace there in after years and finally retired[6] thither to die. His education[7] was entrusted to his two grandfathers, T. Aurelius Fulvus, who, as has been already shown, had enjoyed an honour-

---

[1] *V. P.* 1, 5 and 6.
[2] Hadrian also is said to have had some Spanish blood in him, but this is doubtful. Cf. *V. Hadr.* 1, 1.
[3] *V. P.* 7, 1.   [4] Eutr. viii. 8.   [5] *V. P.* 1, 8.
[6] *V. P.* 12, 6.   [7] *V. P.* 1, 9.

10   THE REIGN OF ANTONINUS PIUS.

able but by no means specially distinguished career, and Arrius Antoninus, who had expressed his pity[1] of Nerva because the latter had been forced to take upon himself the cares of empire. Such were the influences to which Antoninus was in his early life subjected, influences which would induce in him a desire to play a creditable but not a prominent part in Roman politics and to be distinctly averse to the idea of becoming Emperor, if ever such an idea should come within the sphere of possibilities for him. His life was in fact a thorough training for domestic duties[2] but had little of Imperial splendour in it. M. Aurelius[3] alludes to the simplicity of Antoninus's tastes both before and after he had become Emperor, and notes in him the sobriety, truthfulness and reserve, which had been the best characteristics of the Romans of the early Republic. Antoninus's coins[4] too bear in many cases devices illustrative of the legends of Roman mythology, corroborating satisfactorily the view that Antoninus's education was conducted on the most orthodox lines with the purpose of instilling into his mind a devout and simple spirit. His character seems early to have made him a universal favourite, for he inherited[5] the property of many members of his mother's family. His brothers[6] too were dead by 138 A.D., so that he probably inherited the bulk of the property both of his father's and of his mother's family. His estates[7] lay principally at Lorium, while at Lanuvium his family

[1] *V. P.* 1, 4.   [2] *V. P.* 1, 9.   [3] M. Aur. εἰς ἑαυτ. 6, 30.
[4] Cohen, *Ant. P.* 450, 127, 168—175. Eckhel, 7, *Pius's Mythological Coins.*
[5] *V. P.* 1, 9.   [6] *V. P.* 5, 2.   [7] *V. P.* 1, 8.

THE EARLY LIFE OF ANTONINUS.

owned a villa; two lead pipes[1] have also been found at Patavium with the name of Arria Fadilla upon them, which seems to show that Antoninus's mother owned property in that neighbourhood.

Having been born in 86 A.D., Antoninus would assume the Toga virilis[2] at the close of the year 100 A.D. or the commencement of the year 101 A.D., probably at the Liberalia in March 101 A.D., since this festival was the usual if not the invariable occasion of the admission of Roman youths to the dignities of full-grown men. After this he naturally would go through the regular Senatorial "cursus honorum[3]," the Military tribuneship, Vigintiviratus, Quaestorship, Tribuneship, Praetorship and Consulship with one or more of the secondary offices,—such as legatus legionis, legatus Augusti pro praetore, curator aquarum, curator riparum et alvei Tiberis etc.,—which occupied a place in the Senatorial "cursus"; but there is no record of his official career before 121 A.D. except an allusion to his quaestorship, praetorship and consulship.

From Capitolinus[4] we learn that he was "quaestor liberalis, praetor splendidus, consul cum Catilio Severo." Now at this time the qualifications[5] for the quaestorship were:—

    i. Having been *trib. mil. laticlavius* for 1 year[6].
    ii. Having been *xx vir*[7].

---

[1] *C. I. L.* v. 8117 (9).
[2] *V. Marc.* 4, 5. Just. *Inst.* 1, 22. Gaius, 1, 96. Smith's *Dict. Ant.* s.v. Impubes.
[3] Willems, *D. P. R.* 389.
[4] *V. P.* 2, 9.
[5] Willems, *D. P. R.* 433 and 444.
[6] Pliny, *Ep.* iii. 20, 2.
[7] Tac. *Ann.* iii. 29.

12   THE REIGN OF ANTONINUS PIUS.

   iii. Being more than 24 years old[1].
   iv. Being in enjoyment of Senatorial census, free birth and full citizenship.

Such were the qualifications ordinarily demanded in a candidate for the quaestorship; they could indeed be dispensed with in the case of an Imperial favourite, but this Antoninus[2] does not seem to have been. Accordingly Antoninus cannot have been quaestor before 111 A.D. and before this he must have held the office of Trib. mil. laticlavius and XX vir. The qualifications[3] for a seat in the Senate were the same as those for the quaestorship, so that for his admission to the Senate also 111 A.D. is the earliest possible date.

However the quaestorship cannot have fallen much later than this date, as we find him consul[4] with Catilius Severus in 120 A.D., and between these two dates allowance must be made for any of the secondary magistracies that he may have held and also for the praetorship. The epithets of praise bestowed on Antoninus for his tenure of the lower offices—" quaestor liberalis, praetor splendidus "—are significant of what was expected from a magistrate and what his chief business was. His colleague in the consulship—Catilius Severus—is without doubt the individual who is mentioned by the *Scriptores* in two other passages[5]:—" Antonini adoptionem plurimi tunc (138 A.D.) factam esse doluerunt, speciatim Catilius Severus, praefectus urbi, qui sibi praeparabat imperium: qua re prodita successore accepto dignitate privatus est"; and again in the *Life*

---
[1] *Dig.* L. 4, 8.   [2] *V. P.* 6, 10.
[3] Willems, *D. P. R.* 433.   [4] *V. P.* 2, 9. *C. I. L.* viii. 8239.
[5] *V. Hadr.* 24, 6.

of Marcus[1], where Catilius Severus Cos. II, Praef. urbi is mentioned as the great-grandfather of Marcus Aurelius. He was in all probability some ten or more years older than Antoninus, and a man who had played no unimportant part in the government of Rome.

The date of the marriage of Antoninus is uncertain. Marriage was generally but not always early with respectable Romans, that is, before 20 years of age. The wife[2] of Antoninus was Annia Galeria Faustina, the aunt of M. Aurelius, and her brother—M. Aurelius's father—died[3] young, in the year of his praetorship. Accordingly M. Aurelius's father cannot have held the praetorship before 120 A.D., since M. Aurelius was not born[4] till 121 A.D. Now the normal age for the praetorship was about 30 years, so that the birth of M. Aurelius's father may be fairly placed about 90 A.D. and the birth of Annia Galeria Faustina somewhere near the same year. It is then reasonable to imagine that Antoninus married Faustina at some date between 102 and 110 A.D. He married into a good family[5], whose origin like that of his own was provincial; but like his own his wife's family had for several generations been resident in Italy and its members had attained high official position, while alliances had been formed with other distinguished houses. By his marriage Anto-

---

[1] *V. Marc.* 1, 4.   [2] *V. Marc.* 1, 3. *V. P.* 1, 5.
[3] *V. Marc.* 1, 2.   [4] *V. Marc.* 1, 5.
[5] *Genealogical Table of M. Aurelius, V. Marc.* 1, 1—4.

```
Catilius Severus (Cos. ii. Praef. urbi).  Rupilius Bonus  Annius Verus. (Praetorian rank.
   | (V. Hadr. 24, 6) (V. P. 2, 9)           (Cos.)       | From Spain. Made a Senator)
Calvisius Tullius (Cos. ii.)              Rupilia Faustina = Annius Verus. (Cos. ii. Praef. urbi
   |                                                        adscitus in patricios a Vespa-
   |                                                        siano et Tito censoribus)
   |                                         _____|_____
Domitia Calvilla = Annius Verus           Galeria Faustina              Annius Libo (Cos.)
   | (in praetura decessit)               = Antoninus (Pius)
   M. Aurelius Antoninus                  (Annia, V. P. 1, 6)
```

ninus had four children—two sons and two daughters. The sons[1] were M. Aurelius Fulvus Antoninus and M. Galerius Aurelius Antoninus. From the fact that their names appear in the inscriptions of Hadrian's Mausoleum without any list of honours attached to them, it is probable that they died young, but Galerius lived till at least 141 A.D., since his name appears on a coin[2] with that of Diva Faustina, who was not canonized till 141 A.D.:—

{O = M. Γαλέριος 'Αντωνεῖνος Αὐτοκράτορος 'Αντωνείνου υἱὸς
{R = Θεὰ Φαυστεινά.

Antoninus's daughters[3] were Aurelia Fadilla, who married Lamia Silanus, and Galeria Faustina, who married M. Aurelius. The elder daughter died[4] when her father was setting out for the proconsulship of Asia about the year 132 A.D. Now since she was married before this date, it is probable that she was born before 114 A.D.; the younger daughter Galeria Faustina was not married[5] till 146 A.D. and consequently it is unlikely that she was born before 125 A.D. The date of the birth of Antoninus's sons is uncertain but would probably lie between the years 114 A.D. and 125 A.D.

After his consulship in 120 A.D. Antoninus, following the natural inclinations of his character, retired[6] to his country house to lead the quiet life for which he was especially qualified. But he was not allowed to remain for long free from the cares of office. Hadrian, con-

---

[1] *C. I. L.* vi. 988, 989.
[2] Eckhel, 7, *Coins of M. Gal. Aur. Antoninus* and Cohen ii. p. 443.
[3] *C. I. L.* vi. 990. *V. P.* 1, 7. Eutrop. viii. 8.
[4] *V. P.* 3, 6.   [5] *V. Marc.* 6, 6.   [6] *V. P.* 2, 10. Eutr. viii. 8.

vinced of the inability of the Senate to carry on any responsible government, had taken[1] the government of Italy out of the hands of the Senators and had entrusted it in four divisions to *iv viri consulares* appointed by himself. The office must have been one of great importance, especially while Hadrian was absent from Italy on his travels, and though carrying no military power with it, clearly conferred the highest distinction on its holders. A loyal and trustworthy man was required for an office, which might easily become a stepping-stone for an unscrupulous pretender to the Imperial purple. It fell to the lot of Antoninus to become one of these important officers, and he was appointed by Hadrian[2] to the district in which his estates lay, i.e. to Etruria, in which Lorium was situated, with Umbria also in all probability under his command[3]. The story that portents now hailed him as the coming Emperor cannot of course be accepted as historical evidence, but it shows[4] clearly the popular estimation of the importance of his office. That his government in this district of Italy was satisfactory may be inferred from Capitolinus's statement that the reason of Antoninus's adoption by Hadrian was, "cum semper rempublicam bene egisset[5]." How long he held this office is not known. It was not, as we have seen, an office for which many men were fitted, owing to its responsibility and the lack of openings for any ambition consistent with loyalty, and accordingly Antoninus may have held it for several years.

[1] Appian, Ἐμφυλ. 1, 38.
[2] V. P. 2, 11.
[3] Cf. Lacour-Gayet, *Ant. P.* p. 13.
[4] V. P. 3, 1.
[5] V. P. 4, 3.

16 THE REIGN OF ANTONINUS PIUS.

At length between 133 A.D. and 136 A.D.[1] he set out to Asia to hold the proconsulship of that province, but as he started, he lost his elder daughter, the wife of Lamia Silanus[2]. The proconsulship of Asia was the most honourable of all the provincial offices, and following, as it did, in the case of Antoninus on the *iv viratus* of Italy marked him out as one of the very first men in the State, justifying more clearly the portents[3], which subsequent generations found to have accompanied his proconsular rule. In Asia his government earned for him the high praise "that he was the only man to excel his grandfather[4]" and seems to have been the chief reason[5] which induced Hadrian to adopt him; for he showed the steady hand and firm guidance, the serious consideration and the religious application to duty, which were the essentials for a successful tenure of so important an office. He turned his attention principally to the material well-being of his province, and Ionia[6] especially flourished under his rule; Malala[7] mentions buildings of his at Nicomedia in the neighbouring province of Bithynia and at Ephesus, and although these buildings were probably erected during his reign, yet at least they show the keen interest ever

---

[1] Waddington *sur la vie du rhéteur Aristide*, *Mém. de l'Acad.* 1867, shows that the proconsulship of Asia followed 12 to 15 years after the tenure of the consulship, lasting for one year (pp. 218—221, 240—241). Antoninus was Cos. 120 A.D. Therefore his proconsulship falls in some year between 133 A.D. and 136 A.D.

[2] *V. P.* 3, 2; 3, 6.　　　　　[3] *V. P.* 3, 3—5.
[4] *V. P.* 3, 2.　　[5] *V. P.* 4, 3.　　[6] Aristides (Dind.), 1, 363.
[7] Malala (ed. Bonn), xi. p. 281, and cf. *C. I. L.* iii. 324, which refers to the restoration by Diocletian of the Baths of Antoninus at Nicomedia.

felt by Antoninus in the district of which he had once been proconsul. But he could still spare a few moments from his proconsular duties for literary intercourse with such men as Herodes Atticus[1], who was at this time governor of the free cities of Asia and who always enjoyed the friendship of Antoninus[2] in spite of the absurd story mentioned by Philostratus, which states that Herodes Atticus and Antoninus came to blows on the summit of Mt. Ida. Polemon[3] too was resident in the district at Smyrna, an orator or sophist who had had considerable influence with Trajan and Hadrian. Yet his relations with Antoninus were not of the most cordial; for when the proconsul had put up for the night in Smyrna at the house of Polemon in the absence of its owner, the ill-natured sophist returned at midnight and drove the future Emperor into the street.

On his return from the proconsulship between the years 133 A.D. and 136 A.D. Antoninus was admitted to the *Consilium Hadriani*[4], the Imperial cabinet or Privy Council, by whose agency the practical business of the Empire was mainly conducted and whose counsel was taken by the Emperor in all important affairs of state[5]; in this body Antoninus soon gained the reputation of always advocating mild measures. This was the last step in his advancement, before the death of L. Aelius Verus opened to him the path to the throne. Antoninus now held the position of adviser to the Emperor Hadrian and was a leading member of the Senate; he had had the opportunity of understanding the claims

---

[1] Philostr. *v. Sophist.* 2, 555.   [2] *V. Marc.* 2, 4.
[3] Philostr. *v. Sophist.* 1, 534.   [4] *V. P.* 3, 8.
[5] *Vide* chap. 5, § 4.

and pretensions of the Senate while holding the unpopular *iv viratus*, which superseded the Senatorial government of Italy. The position which he now enjoyed was calculated to bring before him still more clearly all the hopes and aspirations of that august body, of which he was himself a member. Nor was the lesson thrown away upon him, since he conferred—when Emperor—as much power on the Senate as he himself had wished to hold when an ordinary Senator[1].

The path to the throne was now opening before Antoninus. He was, as we have seen, clearly one of the leading men of Rome; leading not by virtue of his personal ambition, but owing to the intrinsic worth of his character and to the excellent manner in which he discharged all the duties of government which were entrusted to him. Yet it was not to Antoninus but to L. Aelius Verus that Hadrian first looked when seeking for an Emperor to succeed him. The full name of this Verus, who is called Helius by the *Scriptores Historiae Augustae*, appears to have been[2] Lucius Aurelius Ceionius Commodus Annius Verus, while the name Aelius was added when he passed by adoption into Hadrian's family. He was of a noble Italian[3] family, which came on the father's side[4] from Etruria, from Faventia[5] on the mother's side. His father-in-law Nigrinus had plotted against Hadrian[6] and had been put to death

---

[1] *V. P.* 6, 5.   [2] *V. Hel.* 2, 7.
[3] *Genealogical table of L. Aelius Verus.*

Nigrinus   L. Aurelius Ceionius Commodus Annius Verus (*v. Hel.* 2, 7).

Daughter = L. *Aur. Ceionius Comm. Ann. Aelius Verus* (*v. Hel.* 2, 6—10 adopted by Hadrian), d. 137 A.D. or 138 A.D.
M. Aurelius Antoninus

Lucilla = L. Aur. Ceion. Comm. Ann. Verus Antoninus (*v. Hadr.* 24, 1, adopted by Pius *v. Hel.* 2, 9), Emperor with M. Aurelius.
(*v. Ver.* 2, 4.)

[4] *V. Hel.* 2, 6—8.   [5] *V. Ver.* 1, 9.   [6] *V. Hadr.* 23, 10 and 7, 2.

against that Emperor's wish. There was probably no natural relationship between the family of this L. Aelius Verus and the families of Antoninus (Pius) and M. Aurelius Antoninus. The names are indeed similar, but this similarity means nothing, for the *Scriptores Historiae Augustae* finding the lower members of a family called by certain names would ascribe the same names to their ancestors quite irrespective of whether the names came by adoption or by birth. Moreover the origin of the three families[1] was respectively Italian, Gallic and Spanish; and without doubt, if they had been connected, some direct reference would have been made to the fact.

Hadrian first adopted[2] L. Aelius Verus as his successor, but the latter died[3] in 137 or 138 A.D. having already shown that he was unworthy to rule[4]. He left a young son, too young[5] to be himself adopted as succeeding Emperor, while Marcus Aurelius[6], who was born April 26, 121 A.D., was not yet 17 years old. Accordingly Hadrian, whose health was fast failing him, had to look elsewhere for a man qualified by personal popularity and by experience in public affairs to take on himself the Imperial purple at short notice. Antoninus had qualified himself for Imperial power in both these respects, and the thoughts of Hadrian turned towards him; so that at the beginning of the year 138 A.D. Antoninus[7] was offered the chance of being adopted by Hadrian as his successor. But as the matter was one of great importance, he was allowed some space of time

---

[1] *V. Hel.* 2, 8; *V. P.* 1, 1; *V. Marc.* 1, 2.   [2] *V. P.* 4, 1.
[3] *V. Hel.* 6, 9.   [4] *V. Hadr.* 23, 14.   [5] *V. Ver.* 2, 3.
[6] *V. Marc.* 1, 5 and 5, 1.   [7] *V. P.* 4, 1—4.

for consideration. After due deliberation Antoninus accepted the proffered honour and was adopted by Hadrian, the adoption[1] being an "adrogatio" because he was already "sui iuris." This adoption took place on[2] Feb. 25, 138 A.D. The assertion, gravely contradicted by Capitolinus[3], that the adoption was due to the fact that Hadrian saw Antoninus assisting his father-in-law, Annius Verus, to walk to the Senate-house, is of course nonsense, since many weighty reasons have already been given, which compelled Hadrian to adopt Antoninus. But the adoption of Antoninus was coupled[4] with two other adoptions—those of Marcus, the nephew of Antoninus, and of Lucius Ceionius Commodus, the son of the late L. Aelius Verus. Aelius Spartianus and Julius Capitolinus contradict[5] both themselves and each other in ascribing the adoption of Lucius now to Antoninus, now to Marcus. The confusion arises owing to the youth of Lucius, who was only 7 years old[6] in 138 A.D., and to the fact that he played little part in politics under Antoninus. Hadrian probably insisted on his adoption by Antoninus in order to compensate the family of the Commodi, who had just lost one chance of supplying an Emperor by the death of Lucius' father. Inscriptions[7] prove conclusively that both Marcus and Lucius were adopted by Antoninus. Hadrian had designed Lucius[8] as husband for Annia Galeria Faustina, the younger daughter of Antoninus, but this plan was

---

[1] Willems, *D. P. R.* 67.   [2] *V. P.* 4, 6.
[3] *V. P.* 4, 3.   [4] *V. P.* 4, 4—6.
[5] Ael. Spart. *V. Hadr.* 24, 1 and *V. Hel.* 5, 12; Jul. Capit. *V. Pii,* 4, 5 and *V. Veri,* 2, 2.
[6] *V. Veri,* 2, 10 and 11.   [7] *C. I. L.* 2, 47; *C. I. G.* 1968.
[8] *V. Ver.* 2, 2.

upset soon after Hadrian's death, and Lucius[1] in the end consoled himself with Lucilla, the daughter of Marcus.

Accepting the terms of the adoption Antoninus was adopted[2] Feb. 25, 138 A.D.—not very welcome to him this adoption we may suppose—and judging by the fact that he was already well on in years and that Hadrian provided him with two successors, it is possible to conclude that Hadrian regarded him in the light of a harmless stop-gap, who would be dead by the time Marcus and Lucius were ready for rule. However Hadrian recommended[3] him warmly to the Senate and Antoninus[4] returned thanks for the kind way in which Hadrian had spoken of him. Xiphilinus and Zonaras[5] in their respective abridgements of Dio Cassius give what seems to be a part of this "commendatio," or perhaps of a similar one addressed to the "amici Caesaris," since Xiphilinus speaks of "πρώτους καὶ ἀξιολόγους τῶν βουλευτῶν" as being assembled on that occasion. "Fate," says Hadrian according to Zonaras, "Fate has taken Lucius from us, but I have found you an Emperor, noble, mild, obedient, sensible, neither headstrong and rash through youth nor careless through old age—Antoninus Aurelius." Xiphilinus records a similar speech and adds, "Pius has been educated in accordance with the laws and has held office, so that he will not be ignorant of the duties of an Emperor. Although he is a man who rather shuns politics, and is not desirous of Empire, yet he will consent to rule even against his inclinations." Both

---

[1] *V. Ver.* 2, 4.   [2] *V. P.* 4, 6.
[3] *V. Hadr.* 26, 6.   [4] *V. P.* 4, 6.
[5] Zon. xi. P. 1, 591 c; Xiph. 69. 20, 4.

Zonaras and Xiphilinus[1] say that the adoption of Marcus and Lucius was due to the fact that Antoninus had no sons of his own living, but this statement has been shown to be wrong by a coin already quoted.

Having now been adopted by Hadrian, Antoninus was at the same time, apparently by decree of the Senate, made the colleague[2] of his adoptive father in the Proconsulare Imperium and the Tribunicia Potestas. But though changing his position he did not change the integrity of his character, and his wife, who wished to get some practical profit from her husband's advance, received the rebuke, "Stulta, postquam ad imperium transivimus, et illud, quod habuimus antea, perdidimus." In the words of Eutropius[3], "Vixit ingenti honestate privatus, maiori in imperio," and he increased his sense of honour and of duty with his increase of power and responsibility. Marcus Aurelius[4] testifies that Antoninus had set the example of preserving when Emperor the simple character and simple tastes of a private citizen. "Be firm like him, of an equal temperament, pious, cheerful, kind, a despiser of empty glory, careful, accurate, diligent and thorough. Bear blame and censure from others, as he did; neither hurry nor delay, and let your tastes be simple."

During the four and a half months between Antoninus's adoption and Hadrian's death Antoninus was the actual ruler of the state. We have seen that Hadrian's health[5] was fast failing; he now seems to have become practically mad. In his pain he tried to

---

[1] Xiph. 69. 21, 1; Zon. xi. P. 1, 591 c.
[2] *V. P.* 4, 7. [3] Eutr. viii. 8.
[4] M. Aur. εἰς ἑαυτ. 6, 30. [5] *V. Hadr.* 24, 8—13.

THE EARLY LIFE OF ANTONINUS.

kill himself, but Antoninus prevented him; then he ordered the servant, who had betrayed the design of suicide, to be put to death, but Antoninus[1] saved the man, and was ever on the watch to keep Hadrian from harming himself or others. Such conduct on the part of Antoninus might reasonably have won for him the respect and esteem of all classes, yet we find a wide feeling of discontent[2] with his adoption, a feeling in which Catilius Severus[3] was the leader. He was an ancestor of M. Aurelius on the mother's side and had been twice consul—once with Antoninus in 120 A.D.— and also *praefectus urbi*, and appears to have regarded himself as a likely successor to Hadrian. However, the discontent does not seem to have gone beyond words, for the only notice taken of it was to deprive Catilius of his office of *praefectus urbi*.

Antoninus had tended Hadrian most assiduously, watching over him as a special Providence to save him from his worse self. His dutiful attention is noticed by Capitolinus[4] in the words "et patri cum advixerit, religiosissime paruit." Yet he was the colleague[5] of Hadrian in the two chief Imperial powers—the Procos. Imperium and the Trib. Pot.—and his name appears on the coins[6] of the spring of 138 A.D.:—

$\begin{cases} O = \text{Imp. T. Ael. Caes. Antoninus. (Head bare.)} \\ R = \end{cases}$ i. Hadrianus Aug. Cos. III. P. P. (Head bare.)
or ii. Pietas Trib. Pot. Cos. (woman at altar, right hand holding incense).
or iii. Trib. Pot. Cos. s.c.

[1] *V. P.* 2, 4.   [2] *V. Hadr.* 24, 6 and 7.
[3] *V. Marc.* 1, 4; *V. P.* 2, 9; Xiph. 69. 21, 1; Zon. xi. P. 1, 591 c.
[4] *V. P.* 5, 1.   [5] *V. P.* 4, 7.
[6] Eckhel, *Doct. Numm.* 7 ad ann. and Cohen ii. p. 407.

Here the omission of Augustus after Antoninus's name and the presence of Hadrian's head on the reverse show that Antoninus is not yet Emperor. The word "Pietas" is significant; his characteristic virtue had been already observed, but the name of Pius had not yet been bestowed upon him. Doubtless Antoninus now acted as Emperor, while Hadrian was mad, giving up the power again in the latter's sane moments. Towards the end, however, Hadrian in a momentary lull of his disease went away to Baiae[1] for the hot weather, leaving Antoninus as ruler in Rome. But in the beginning of July 138 A.D. Antoninus was summoned to Baiae to the death-bed of Hadrian and left young Marcus[2] to look after his interests in Rome, and to do what was necessary in honour of Hadrian. Hadrian died[3] at Baiae on July 10, 138 A.D., and there was no difficulty now in Antoninus, who had already been the acting Emperor, succeeding at once to the nominal position also.

[1] *V. Hadr.* 25, 5 and 6.   [2] *V. Marc.* 6, 1.   [3] *V. Hadr.* 25, 6.

CHAPTER III.

REIGN OF ANTONINUS PIUS TILL 148 A.D.

ANTONINUS entered on his difficult task of ruling the Roman Empire on July 10, 138 A.D., and his first care was for the memory[1] of Hadrian. He brought the body of the late Emperor from Baiae to Rome with all due solemnity and respect and laid it to rest in the gardens of Domitia, which sloped down from the north side of the Mons Janiculus round the bend of the Tiber till they came opposite the Campus Martius. In these gardens lay the Mausoleum Hadriani which Hadrian[2] had built for himself, because there was no further room[3] in the Mausoleum Augusti; Capitolinus[4] ascribes this new Mausoleum to Antoninus, and he may have put the finishing touches to Hadrian's work. The statement however that Hadrian was buried at Puteoli[5] is no doubt a mistake, since there is no support for it outside the *Scriptores Historiae Augustae*, while there is evidence both within these authors and beyond them that he was buried in the Mausoleum across the Tiber.

At any rate there was little regret and no small satisfaction at the death of an Emperor[6] whose life by

---

[1] *V. P.* 5, 1.   [2] Xiph. 69. 23, 1.   [3] *V. Hadr.* 19, 11.
[4] *V. P.* 8, 2.   [5] *V. Hadr.* 25, 7.   [6] *V. Hadr.* 25, 7.

its closing scenes had won for him the ill-will of all; it was now the endeavour of Antoninus to remove the bad impression caused by the last few months of Hadrian's reign and to restore his memory to popularity. He therefore procured a pardon[1] from the Senate for those whom Hadrian had condemned, saying that such would have been Hadrian's own action, if he had lived. But the Senate was by no means inclined to honour the memory of a dead man, who in his lifetime had condemned[2] many Senators and had set up the unpopular *iv viri*[3] in Italy, who had lived for the greater part of his reign out of Rome and had exalted the provinces at the expense of the Imperial city[4]. The Senators were at first resolved not to pass the formal ratification of the *Acta Hadriani*[5] nor to give him divine honours[6]. But if they had refused the former, they would theoretically have made invalid[7] all the acts of Hadrian and have caused an impossible confusion in political, social and financial affairs. Probably a compromise was arrived at by Antoninus agreeing to the reversal of some of the most obnoxious acts, such as the condemnation of some of Hadrian's victims, and consenting[8] to the abolition of the *iv viri* in Italy. Antoninus however found more difficulty[9] in obtaining divine honours for Hadrian. All classes

---

[1] *V. P.* 6, 3.

[2] *V. Hadr.* 15, 3—8; Xiph. 70, 1, 2; Zon. xii. P. 1, 592 D (ἄνδρες ἐπιφανέστατοι).

[3] Appian, Ἐμφ. 1, 38.

[4] Hadrian was also unpopular with the Senate on account of his exalting the Equites. Cf. Schurz, *de Mutat. in imp. R. ord. ab imp. Hadr. fact.*, pp. 29, 30. [5] *V. Hadr.* 27, 1—2. [6] *V. P.* 5, 1.

[7] Willems, *D. P. R.* 411. [8] *V. Marc.* 11, 6. [9] *V. P.* 5, 1.

in the State with but few exceptions resisted this; and it was not until Antoninus had most earnestly entreated the Senate and had threatened[1] to refuse to rule unless they complied, that the Senate, principally out of respect for the petitioner and partly through fear of the soldiers with whom Hadrian had been popular, acceded to Antoninus's request and canonized Hadrian. Antoninus[2] thereupon instituted an order of priests in honour of Hadrian and dedicated a magnificent shield to him. From this time onward "Divus Hadrianus" is found on inscriptions referring to Hadrian and he received a recognized place among the deities of Rome, his priests being the "sodales Hadrianales[3]" parallel to the Augustales, Claudiales, Flaviales etc. Inscriptions[4] are found alluding to the worship of the Genii of Emperors generally and in particular to a provision for the maintenance of priests and appliances for the worship of Divus Hadrianus at Rome. A temple[5] too was soon begun in honour of Hadrian which was dedicated in 145 A.D. and restored or enlarged in 151 A.D. Thus at last all was done that duty could suggest or piety require for the honouring of Hadrian's name and memory.

The humble manner in which Antoninus had petitioned the Senate must have been very reassuring to that body after the arbitrary way in which it had been treated by Hadrian; it was significant of Anto-

---

[1] Xiph. 70. 1, 2; Zon. xii. P. 1, 593 A. [2] V. P. 5, 2.
[3] C. I. L. vi. 1408, 1409; C. I. L. x. 3724, 4750.
[4] C. I. L. vi. 253, 254.
[5] V. P. 8, 2; V. Veri, 3, 1; Eckhel, 7, ad ann. 151 A.D. *N.B. for date* 145 A.D. *vide infra ad ann.*

ninus's habitual policy of consulting and deferring to the Senate as much as possible and of never actually forcing it. The Senate now showed that its former obstinacy had not been due to ill-will towards Antoninus himself. Antoninus had of course assumed the title of Augustus immediately after Hadrian's death and had taken on himself the fitting office of Pontifex Maximus[1], always reserved at this time for the Emperor. The Senate now bestowed the title of Augusta[2] on his wife Annia Galeria Faustina, while for the Emperor himself it found a new and appropriate name—*Pius*,—a name which first appears on the coins[3] of the autumn of 138 A.D. in conjunction with the title "Cos. Des. II":—

> O = Imp. Caes. T. Ael. Caes. Hadri. Antoninus. (Head bare or wreathed.)
> R = Aug. Pius, P. M. Tr. P. Cos. Des. II. s.c. (Woman with bough in right hand, in her left a cornucopia.)

The historians are needlessly agitated to find the correct reason for this name of Pius. Capitolinus[4] gives his readers the choice among five reasons:— (i) He supported his aged father-in-law with his arm in presence of the Senate. (ii) He saved those whom Hadrian had ordered for execution. (iii) He was persistent in his demand for divine honours for Hadrian. (iv) He prevented Hadrian committing suicide. (v) He was clement and kind. Eutropius[5] says "Pius propter clementiam dictus est." Suidas[6] says he was so-called ἐκ τοῦ ἤθους, and Pausanias[7] finds the reason in his

---

[1] Eckhel, 7, ad ann. 138 A.D.   [2] V. P. 5, 2.
[3] Eckhel, 7, ad ann. 138 A.D. and Cohen, 66—80.   [4] V. P. 2, 3—7.
[5] Eutrop. viii. 8.   [6] Suidas, s.v. Antoninus.   [7] Paus. 8. 43, 5.

devout worship of the gods. Aelius Spartianus[1] allows us our choice of three causes:—(i) because he supported his father-in-law; (ii) because he saved many senators from the outbursts of Hadrian's frenzy; (iii) because he obtained honours for Hadrian. Orosius[2] says that he governed the State in such a peaceful and holy spirit that he was rightly called Pius and the Father of his country; while Xiphilinus and Zonaras[3] agree in stating that he received the name of Pius because, when he became Emperor, many men were lying under sentence and Antoninus refused to stain the commencement of his reign by enforcing such punishments.

Leaving out the statement of Orosius, which is very much like being wise after the event, we may say that all the reasons are correct. If any technical justification of the name "Pius" be required, it may be found in the tenderness of Antoninus to his father-in-law and his solicitous care for his adoptive father. But more widely than this it finds a complete justification in the kindred notions of duty, respect for justice and for the immoveable ἄγραπτα νόμιμα of right and wrong, and in the kindly feeling of kinship with all, which were the noble characteristics of Antoninus.

Beyond this name of Pius, Antoninus received by decree[4] statues in honour of his father, mother and brothers who were already dead, and accepted them gladly; he allowed *Ludi Circenses* to be fixed for the anniversary of his birthday, Sept. 19, but other honours he declined for the present. To *circenses*[5] he was always

---

[1] *V. Hadr.* 24, 3—5.   [2] Orosius, 7. 14, 1.
[3] Xiph. 70. 2, 1; Zon. xii. P. 1, 593 A.   [4] *V. P.* 5, 2.
[5] *V. P.* 10, 9.

greatly attached and seems to have been a thorough Roman in his liking for the pageants of the theatre and amphitheatre[1]. Among other honours which he probably refused at this period was the title of Pater Patriae, which he accepted in 139 A.D., after one refusal[2]. He was, in the words of M. Aurelius[3], no lover of empty glory and preferred to hold no title which he had not clearly earned.

We have seen how Antoninus Pius deferred to the Senate and how the Senators were not afraid to offer a resistance to his entreaties. He himself had long been one of them and had lived among them once with no prospect of ever rising to a higher position. He could therefore fully sympathize with all their hopes and claims and was willing to allow them not only a nominal but even a real power, if they were able to use it[4]. Certainly then—with the exception of individual members like Catilius Severus, whose private ambitions had been disappointed,—the whole Senate must have welcomed gladly his accession to empire. The provinces had yet hardly received the news of the change of Emperor, or at least had not had time to act upon the news; but already at Patrae[5] in Achaia a statue to Antoninus Pius was set up by L. Gallius Menander Iustus, while at Aquincum[6] in Pannonia Inferior a dedication was made to his Genius by and at the expense of the Collegium Augustale of the town, C. Iulius Crescens being the prime mover in the matter,

[1] Cf. M. Corn. Fronto, *de Feriis Alsiniensibus*, p. 226.
[2] *V. P.* 6, 6; Eckhel, 7, ad ann. 139 A.D. and Cohen, 21.
[3] M. Aur. εἰς ἑαυτ. 6, 30.   [4] *V. P.* 6, 5.
[5] *C. I. L.* iii. 501.   [6] *C. I. L.* iii. 3487.

—a dedication which must be assigned to this year, since the titles subsequently conferred on Antoninus Pius are omitted in the inscription. Then too at Hatne not far from Damascus and at Perinthus in Thrace inscriptions[1] of this year are found in honour of Antoninus.

Thus the provinces, naturally very friendly to Hadrian who had visited almost every part of his Empire, hastened to welcome the man whom Hadrian had chosen as his successor. Nor was Italy behindhand, for an inscription of this year has been found at Sipontum[2] which commemorates some dedication to Antoninus. What the populace of Rome thought of their new ruler is not known, but the minor officials in Rome, such as the Viatores of the Imperial, Consular and Praetorian courts and the Scribae Armamentarii[3], certainly welcomed him at once, either with the design of winning his favour or from gratitude that his accession did not involve their removal. No class indeed throughout the Empire can have found any occasion for blame in a man whose life hitherto had been marked by a kindliness, truth and justice, which won for him the friendship of all, and who on becoming Emperor did not in any way change his simple character[4]. There was in fact no change of government with the accession of Antoninus,—none at least in the provinces,—while in Rome and Italy there were some alterations for the better. Capitolinus[5] states that Antoninus Pius superseded none of those whom Hadrian had promoted, re-

---

[1] *C. I. L.* iii. 131, 780.
[2] *C. I. L.* ix. 697.
[3] *C. I. L.* vi. 998, 999.
[4] M. Aur. εἰς ἑαυτ. 6, 30.
[5] *V. P.* 5, 3.

ferring especially to the provincial governors; Aristides[1] confirms this, saying that Pius had begun his rule without causing any of the wrongs or disturbances, which are an incidental and in some degree an inevitable evil consequent on the change of rulers.

There is still one other point to which reference must be made before we pass on to the year 139 A.D. Hadrian[2] had provided that Lucius, the young adoptive son of Antoninus Pius, should marry Galeria Faustina, Antoninus's younger daughter, while M. Aurelius[3] was to marry Lucius's sister, the daughter of the late L. Aelius Verus; but owing to the youth of Lucius[4]—he was now in his 8th year—and doubtless also to the affection of Antoninus Pius for Marcus, this arrangement was set aside and Galeria Faustina was betrothed to Marcus[5], the marriage taking place in 146 A.D., after Marcus's second consulship. Having thus made new arrangements for his daughter's marriage, Antoninus Pius became Cos. Des. II for the succeeding year with C. Bruttius Praesens as his colleague designate, who had himself held the consulship before.

The year 139 A.D. opens with the consulship[6] of Imp. Caesar T. Aelius Hadrianus Antoninus Augustus Pius II and C. Bruttius Praesens II. The consulship being an office which the Emperors held only from time to time, the new tenure of the consulship by Antoninus Pius would naturally begin with the beginning of the year, since the first consulship of the year

---

[1] Arist. εἰς βασ. (Dind.) 1, 100.　　　[2] V. Veri, 2, 3.
[3] V. Marc. 4, 5.　　　[4] V. Marc. 6, 2.
[5] V. Marc. 6, 5—6; Eutrop. viii. 10; V. P. 1, 7; 10, 2.
[6] C. I. G. 3175; C. I. L. iii. p. 937.

REIGN OF ANTONINUS PIUS TILL 148 A.D.

was eponymous[1] and consequently brought more distinction with it. Whether Antoninus renewed his Tribunicia Potestas at the commencement of each succeeding year is another question. His first Tribunicia Potestas began on Feb. 25, 138 A.D., and thus if he held this power in yearly terms reckoning from Feb. 25, his second Tr. Pot. began on Feb. 25, 139 A.D. and so on for the other years of his reign. Eckhel however believes that he renewed this power on Jan. 1 each year and quotes a coin of 161 A.D., which bears Tr. Pot. XXIIII upon it. Now Pius died early in March 161 A.D. and hence Eckhel[2] assumes that the Tr. Pot. was renewed at the commencement of the year, since it would be unlikely that new coins would be struck between Feb. 25 and the first days of March. But it is perfectly possible for coins to have been struck at that period, since preparations for the new coinage would have to be made some time before and the new coins would probably be issued punctually on Feb. 25. Moreover there are numerous inscriptions which disprove Eckhel's theory. At Sardis[3] and at Athens[4] inscriptions have been found bearing the title Tr. P. II Cos. III, which can only be referred to the period from Jan. 1 to Feb. 25, 140 A.D., when Antoninus's third consulship had begun, while his second Tribunicia Potestas was not yet ended. Similarly at Compsa an inscription has been discovered with Tr. P. Cos. II upon it, which must belong to the beginning of 139 A.D. In Gallia Narbonensis also numerous milestones[5] have

---

[1] Willems, *D. P. R.* 447, 448.
[2] Eckhel, 7, ad ann. 139 A.D. and 161 A.D.   [3] *C. I. G.* 3457.
[4] *C. I. L.* iii. 549.   [5] *C. I. L.* xii. 5533, 5541, 5544, 5603, 5604, etc.

been found bearing on them Tr. P. VII Cos. IIII and consequently are referable only to the commencement of 145 A.D. Eckhel's view must therefore be given up entirely, and Feb. 25 must be accepted as the day for the renewal of the Tr. Pot. by Antoninus each year of his reign.

By the year 139 A.D. information of the succession of Antoninus had reached the furthest limits of the Empire, and sufficient time had passed for the various provinces to take steps to honour their new ruler. One of the customary honours[1] bestowed upon new Emperors was the presentation[2] of the "Aurum Coronarium" from every part of the Empire. Festus (*Triumph. Cor.*) says, "Triumphales coronae sunt, quae imperatori aureae praeferantur, quae temporibus antiquis propter paupertatem laureae fuerunt"; and the Monumentum Ancyranum[3] mentions among the acts of benevolence, for which Augustus claims credit, his generosity in the matter of this Aurum Coronarium. "Auri coronari pondo triginta et quinque millia municipiis et colonis Italiae conferentibus ad triumphos remisi et postea quotienscumque Imperator appellatus aurum coronarium non accepi." From this it is evident that the presentation was always connected with the bestowal of the title Imperator, and it was doubtless so in the case of Antoninus, though Capitolinus[4] connects it with his adoption. Practically it makes no difference which of the two we regard as the right reason for the

---

[1] Willems, *D. P. R.* 470.
[2] This account of the presentation of "aurum coronarium" is drawn mainly from Eckhel, 7, ad ann. 139 A.D.
[3] *Mon. Ancyr.* 4, 26.   [4] *V. P.* 4, 10.

presentation of the "aurum coronarium" to Antoninus, since in his case the title Imperator was conferred on him at his adoption[1]. The crowns were of laurel at first; then golden crowns were substituted for those of laurel, while by the time of Augustus a gift of gold was usually made without the idea of a crown being preserved.

Eckhel[2] is undoubtedly right in referring a series of coins, which bear marked traces of similarity to each other, to this year. They are the coins of various provinces and semi-dependent states, in most of which the obverse is the same, while the reverse bears the name of the district with similar devices on all. It may be interesting to give a description of a few of these coins:—

1. { O = Antoninus Aug. Pius P. P. (Head wreathed.)
     R = Africa s.c. (Woman stands with spoils of elephant beside her, in right hand a casket, in left a cornucopiae. At her feet a lion.)

2. R = Africa Cos. II. s.c. (Woman running with large crown in her hand. At her feet a snake.)

3. R = Alexandria Cos. II. s.c. (Woman with casket in each hand.)

4. { O = Antoninus Aug. Pius P. P. (Head wreathed.)
     R = Asia Cos. II. s.c. (Woman stands with towered head, r. crown, l. anchor. At her feet prow of a ship.)

5. { O = as above.
     R = Cappadocia Cos. II. s.c. (Woman with robe girt up and towered head. r. casket, l. standard. Mt. Argaeus at her feet.)

[1] V. P. 4, 6—7; Eckhel, 7, ad ann. 138 A.D.
[2] Eckhel, 7, ad ann. 139 A.D.; cf. Cohen, 21—28, 551—553.

6. ⎰O = *as above.*
   ⎱R = Dacia Cos. II. S.C. (Woman standing. *r.* crown with spikes, *l.* vexillum.)
7. R = Hispania Cos. II. S.C. (Woman with towered head. *r.* crown, *l.* bough. At her feet some small animal.)
8. R = Mauretania Cos. II. S.C. (Man with robes caught up. *r.* casket, *l.* spear.)

Similar coins are also found for Phoenicia, Sicily, Syria and for Parthia and Scythia. Now all these coins, where they bear a date, are dated to the second consulship of Antoninus, i.e. 139 A.D., and they all bear similar devices, the Genius of the district offering a gift, in some cases a crown, in others a casket suitable for carrying gold or valuables, while in the case of Africa the eagerness of the provincials is shown by the fact that the bearer of the present is running. It is not to be supposed that these coins can refer to the wars of Antoninus, for the British war was the only disturbance of the sort during the early years of this reign. Nor do they refer to the general prosperity and the flourishing condition of the provinces under Pius, as though the whole Empire had suddenly burst into blossom with the accession of the new Emperor. From the fact that

(i) Capitolinus[1] mentions the presentation of Aurum Coronarium to Antoninus,

(ii) 139 A.D. would be about the date of this presentation,

(iii) These coins, all belonging to 139 A.D., all represent various districts offering crowns or the equivalent of crowns,

[1] *V. P.* 4, 10.

—from this we can have no doubt that the coins refer in graphic style to the presentation of the Aurum Coronarium to Antoninus Pius.

It is worthy of note that Parthia and Scythia are represented as making presents to the new Emperor. They were not provinces, but were at this time within the fringe of semi-dependent states, which girdled the Roman Empire,—restless nations[1], who were always waiting for an opportunity of oppressing their neighbours, and who in the time of Antoninus caused disturbances on the Eastern and Northern frontiers. Their action in the present case was prompted by a desire to buy off the interference of the Emperor in their local quarrels.

Of the Aurum Coronarium Antoninus returned half to the provincials and all to the Italians[2]; nor were the inhabitants of Rome itself left in the cold, for from coins[3] of this year it is shown that Antoninus now bestowed his first congiarium on the populace:—

{O = Antoninus Aug. Pius P. P.
{R = Liberalitas P. M. Tr. P. Cos. II. S.C.

(N.B. On Antoninus's coins the number of the Tr. Pot. is not given till 148 A.D. Tr. Pot. XI.)

Capitolinus[4] mentions this gift to the populace and adds that Antoninus gave also "ea quae pater promiserat." It is uncertain whether this refers to any promise of Hadrian to the populace of Rome; but we have abundant evidence that Antoninus fulfilled or supplemented the promises of Hadrian to various town-

---

[1] V. P. 9, 6—9.   [2] V. P. 4, 10.
[3] Eckhel, 7, ad ann. 139 A.D.; Cohen, *Ant. P.* 648, 649.
[4] V. P. 4, 9.

ships of Italy. At Ostia[1] he carried out Hadrian's bequest for the building of baths in that town, adding himself whatever money was required beyond the 20,000 sesterces left by Hadrian for the purpose. The date of this action was probably 139 A.D., for, although the actual date cannot be read on the inscription, there is just room to insert "Tr. Pot. II Cos. II." Again at Puteoli[2] a sea-wall or pier had been washed down by the sea and Hadrian had promised to restore it. Antoninus in 139 A.D. restored it, building a kind of mole or pier resting upon 20 supports to resist the encroachments of the sea. To Signia[3] also Hadrian had given money for public works and had left them something in his will; as far as can be made out from a defective inscription Antoninus supplemented Hadrian's bequest from his own purse. Again at Capua[4] an inscription is found in the amphitheatre stating that Capua built it, Hadrian restored it and added columns, while Antoninus dedicated it; and it appears that he also restored the amphitheatre of Firmum Picenum[5] by means of money bequeathed by Hadrian.

Pius had now earned a warm affection from all classes and conditions of his subjects and the Senate once again urged upon him the acceptance of the title "Pater Patriae[6]," which he had refused before. This time he accepted, expressing the deepest gratitude for the honour conferred upon him. Coins were then struck bearing his new title, while on some of the

---

[1] *C. I. L.* xiv. 98.   [2] *C. I. L.* x. 1640, 1641.
[3] *C. I. L.* x. 5963.   [4] *C. I. L.* x. 3832.
[5] *C. I. L.* x. 5355 and 6078, § 5.   [6] *V. P.* 6, 6.

coins[1] of this year the epithet "optimus princeps" appears.

For the year 140 A.D. Antoninus became consul[2] for the third time, taking at the request of the Senate his adopted son Marcus—now aged 19—as his colleague[3]. In this year for the first time coins of Marcus were struck, some of which refer to his new office, others to his position as *princeps iuventutis*, while a third set refer to his admission to the priestly colleges[4]:—

{O = Aurelius Caes. Aug. Pii F. Cos.
{R =| Honos.
  or | Iuventus. s.c.
  or | Pietas Aug. (with *instrumenta pontificia*)[5].

At some period before the year 140 A.D. the island of Britain was disturbed by an outbreak, the date and incidents of which are very uncertain. Historians give us no clue to the date of the British War and inscriptions very little assistance, so that it is necessary to fall back on the help of coins. It is to be observed that the title Imperator II first occurs on coins[6] between 140 and 143 A.D. fixed to this period by the presence of the title Cos. III, but not to be fixed any more nearly because the number of the Tr. Pot. is not given. Antoninus Pius was Cos. III in 140 A.D., while at the close of 144 A.D. he was Cos. Des. IV. In the British coins of this period the title Imperator II is coupled with the name Britannia, while the design on the coins is generally significant of a victory won; in

---

[1] Eckhel, 7, ad ann. 139 A.D.; and Cohen, 790.
[2] *C. I. L.* xiv. 246, 2795.
[3] *V. P.* 6, 9; *V. Marc.* 1, 5 and 6, 3.   [4] *V. Marc.* 6, 3.
[5] Eckhel, 7, *Coins of M. Aurelius*, 140 A.D.; and Cohen, ii. p. 410.
[6] Eckhel, 7, ad ann. 140—143.

other words the Roman arms had just been successful in Britain at the time the coins[1] were struck.

1. { O = Antoninus Aug. Pius P. P. Tr. P. Cos. III. (Head wreathed.)
   R = Britannia S.C. Imperator II. (Woman sits on rock. r. military standard, l. spear.)
2. R = Imp. II. (Victory sits holding shield inscribed "Britan.")
3. R = Britann. (Victory standing on globe. r. crown.)
4. { O = Antoninus Aug. Pius Tr. P. Cos. III. (Head wreathed.)[2]
   R = Imperator II. Britan. S.C. (Victory on globe. r. wreath, l. ear of corn.)

Undoubtedly then the coins of this period prove that a victory over the Britons had just been gained and undoubtedly the title Imperator II was first given about the same time. It is to be noted that Pius only repeated the title of Imperator once and consequently it may be inferred that he did not take it on any occasion without due cause. Now the title Imperator[3] was really that with which soldiers hailed their leader on the field of a successful battle, though its use had been somewhat extended under the Empire, when Imperator Caesar had been substituted for Caesar Imperator; there is no other war which can be put down to this period and accordingly we are driven to the conclusion that Antoninus assumed the title Imperator II at this period in honour of his victory over the Britons. An inscription[4] has been found containing the titles "Tr. P. II, Imp. II, Cos. II, Des. III,"

---

[1] Eckhel, *l.c.*; cf. Cohen, 113 and 114.   [2] Cohen, 500.
[3] Willems, *D. P. R.* p. 406, n. 3.   [4] *Marm. Grut.*, p. 253, 7.

REIGN OF ANTONINUS PIUS TILL 148 A.D.

which though unsupported by parallel cases cannot be assumed to be false. Eckhel[1] considers it to be a mistake, but there is no reason why it should not be genuine and in default of other evidence it must be trusted. This inscription proves that Antoninus was hailed Imperator for the second time in 139 A.D.; but since no other inscriptions of 139 A.D. give Antoninus this title and since the title does not appear on coins before 140 A.D., it is probable that the victory over the Britons and the subsequent bestowal of the new title did not take place till the end of 139 A.D. The date 139 A.D. is supported by the fact that on the coins of 139 A.D. Britain[2] is not one of the provinces that present the "aurum coronarium." The "argumentum ex silentio" is of course a very doubtful one, but it may show that Britain was at this time too much disturbed with war to pay that respect to the Emperor, which, as Eckhel shows, was paid by other provinces at the beginning of 139 A.D.

As to the war itself we know very little. Pausanias[3] says that the Brigantes in Britain ventured to invade Genunia, which was subject to the Romans, and that in consequence they were deprived of most of their land. The Brigantes lived both to the north and to the south of Hadrian's Wall, while the locality of Genunia is unknown. Capitolinus[4] is more general than Pausanias and only states that Antoninus Pius conquered the Britons by means of his legate Lollius Urbicus and removed the barbarians, building a wall of turf.

These statements seem to show that it was not

[1] Eckhel, 7, ad ann. 140—143 A.D. [2] Cf. Eckhel, quoted above.
[3] Paus. 8. 43, 4. [4] *V. P.* 5, 4.

an invasion from Caledonia but an outbreak of the nominally dependent tribe of the Brigantes, who overran the district south of their territory and were in consequence removed to the north of the Forth and Clyde. It cannot have been a very serious campaign for Rome, probably guerilla warfare with no pitched battles; drawings[1] of a boar running occur on several inscriptions of the period, which may point to the fact that the war was rather the hunting of rebels than the meeting of armies. Yet it was serious enough to occasion the taking of vows to Juppiter, Fortune and other gods and goddesses, and it probably dragged on for at least a year through a course of skirmishes, flights, rallyings and defeats, until the disturbance was finally quelled and vows could be paid " ob res trans vallum prospere gestas[2]."

The general to whom the war was entrusted was the legate of the province Q. Lollius Urbicus[3], whose family came from Tiddis in Prov. Numidia, of which town he was patron, and who after holding various minor offices at Rome had served with distinction under Hadrian in the Jewish war and had held the governorships of Germania Inferior and of Asia. The general was a man of no little experience and he used his success in this war as a stepping-stone to further honours, if we may judge from the fact that he afterwards became proconsul of Africa and Praefectus urbi[4]. The labour of the war—whatever it was—seems to have been done thoroughly; for at Carridden in Lin-

---

[1] *C. I. L.* vii. 1133, 1133 a, 1137. [2] *C. I. L.* vii. 940.
[3] *C. I. L.* viii. 6706; *V. P.* 5, 4.
[4] Appuleius, *Apol.* 381; Fronto, *ad amicos*, 2, 7; *C. I. L.* viii. 6705.

lithgowshire we find an inscription[1] to Antoninus with a drawing representing an armed horseman brandishing his spear over four captives, who lie at his feet, their weapons thrown aside, while the head of one captive has been struck off. Again at Duntocher[2] there is a representation of Mars standing victorious, while by his side are two winged Victories poised on globes and a figure bearing a vexillum, on which "Virt. Aug." (virtus Augusta) is inscribed. At Castlehill[3] near Glasgow is a figure of Victory holding a garland, while near her is a scene similar to that described in *C. I. L.* vii. 1088.

As a result of the war the Brigantes were deprived of that part of their land which lay south of the Forth and Clyde and were removed *en masse* to the north of these rivers[4]. To secure the southern district another wall was built north of Hadrian's wall stretching across the 40 miles space which separates the estuaries of the Forth and Clyde. There were already some defences at this spot, for its advantages as a line of defence could not have escaped the well-trained eye of Domitian's general Agricola. Tacitus[5] refers to these works and their purpose in words similar to those used by Capitolinus in respect of Antoninus's wall. But these defences must have been practically given up or Hadrian would hardly have built another wall so much further to the south.

The soldiers of Legio XX Valeria victrix, Legio VI

---

[1] *C. I. L.* vii. 1088.   [2] *C. I. L.* vii. 1135.   [3] *C. I. L.* vii. 1130.
[4] *V. P.* 5, 4; Paus. 8. 43, 4.
[5] Tac. *Agr.* 23, "the space is narrow between Clota and Bodotria:— quod tum praesidiis firmabatur atque omnis propior sinus tenebatur summotis velut in aliam insulam hostibus."

victrix, pia fidelis, and Legio II Augusta were employed under the superintendence of Q. Lollius Urbicus in constructing the new wall[1], which was built mainly of turf[2]. Stuart[3] in his account of the wall from observation of the remains gives as his belief that there was first a ditch 40 ft. wide and 20 ft. deep, on the north side; then came the second line of defence—a mound 20 ft. high and 24 ft. thick at the base, fortified with small towers and flanked on the south by a military road; further south there was a chain of forts 18 or 19 in number. Hübner[4] from a comparison of the inscriptions found in the neighbourhood shows that there were 10 towers in the wall itself in localities whose names now are Rough Castle, Castle Cary, Westerwood, Barhill, Auchindavie, Kirkintilloch, Belmulie, Castlehill, Duntocher and West Kilpatrick[5].

Antoninus Pius received the title Imperator II as a result of this war, but it is doubtful whether he enjoyed a triumph; Eckhel quotes a coin which seems to point to a triumph at this period:—

{O = Antoninus Aug. Pius P. P. (Head wreathed.)
{R = Tr. Pot. Cos. II. (Emperor in chariot with 2 small figures probably representing Marcus and Lucius.)

On the other hand S. Aurelius Victor definitely says that Pius never actually triumphed and though not

[1] *C. I. L.* vii. 1125, 1130, 1133, 1135.
[2] "Cespiticium," *V. P.* 5, 4. [3] Stuart, *Caledonia Romana.*
[4] *C. I. L.* vii. pp. 191, 192.
[5] W. M. Ramsay (*Athenæum, July* 15 *and* 29, 1893) says that the ditch was a considerable and varying distance from the wall, which was not more than 10 ft. or 14 ft. thick at the base. The ditch was only a *Limes,* and the wall and road a means of easy communication between the forts and to some extent a screen from observation.

much faith must be put in Victor[1], yet it is safer to suppose that Antoninus triumphed neither now nor at any other time.

It was probably in the course of the year 140 A.D. that the attention of the Roman World was directed towards the East by a disaster which befell the south-west corner of Asia Minor and the adjacent islands, an earthquake in which Rhodes was the principal sufferer.

During the reign of Antoninus Pius there were at least two distinct earthquakes, which made themselves felt over the western part of Asia Minor. Aristides alone mentions two distinct shocks and he mentions them in different places, so that he might be thought to have given two accounts of the same occurrence, if the dates and localities referred to did not prevent any such hypothesis. With regard to the first shock Aristides[2] states that Rhodes was destroyed at the time when he was in Egypt, while from another passage[3] we know that he was a friend of Heliodorus, who was prefect of Egypt for some period extending from the beginning of Antoninus's reign to some years after 140 A.D.[4] It is probable that Aristides's visit to Egypt would be made when his friend was prefect, and in consequence 140 A.D. may be fixed as a fairly approximate date for the first earthquake. Rhodes is the only place certainly mentioned as being overwhelmed by this earthquake, but as Aristides[5] states that Mitylene, Ephesus and Smyrna suffered at another time, and since the places which are mentioned elsewhere as suffering by earth-

---

[1] S. Aur. Vict., *De Caess.* 15.
[2] Arist. (Dind.) 1, 824.
[3] Arist. (Dind.) 1, 524.
[4] *C. I. G.* 4955.
[5] Arist. (Dind.) 1, 497.

quake in Antoninus's reign may be divided clearly into two groups by their geographical position, it may be confidently asserted that the first earthquake—occurring in 140 A.D. or about that time—affected the south-west corner of Asia Minor including Cos, Rhodes, Caria, Lycia and the west of Pisidia, while the second shock—occurring about 151 or 152 A.D.—affected the north-west corner including Ephesus, Smyrna, Mitylene, Cyzicus, Nicomedia and Bithynia[1].

Aristides[2] in his Ῥοδιακὸς gives a graphic description of the destruction of Rhodes by the first shock;—"when the earthquake was coming upon the island, the sea retreated and left the harbours dry; houses and tombs were rent asunder and thrown down; tower fell on tower, dockyard on trireme, temples on altars, men on men. While a man might have been weighing anchor to set sail, the disaster came, and before he could have looked round, the city was swallowed up."

"The beauty[3] of the harbours is gone, their glory departed; the temples are empty of treasures, the altars of sacrifices, the race-courses and theatres of men. No trace remains of the dockyards; all the countless statues are lost, dashed to pieces and destroyed with all the ivory and gold. The whole wealth of Rhodes has vanished, disorder reigns supreme and a disaster has happened equalled by none within our memory."

Capitolinus[4] mentions that Rhodes and the cities of Asia suffered and Pausanias[5] confirms this, picking out Rhodes and Cos as the chief sufferers. From inscrip-

---

[1] *Vide* account of second earthquake, 151—152 A.D. *infra*.
[2] Arist. (Dind.) 1, 804.   [3] Arist. (Dind.) 1, 800.
[4] *V. P.* 9, 1.   [5] Paus. 8. 43, 4.

tions[1] it appears that the devastation was great at Stratonicea in Caria; in this town the temple of Dionysus[2] was overthrown and the destruction was so universal that one of the inhabitants made a dedication to Antoninus Pius in gratitude at being spared in so great a calamity. Cyaneae in Lycia was also affected, and an inscription[3] is found set up by the senate and people of this town in the governorship of C. Corn. Proculus thanking Pius for his assistance in the time of need, while in 147 A.D. Velia Procula[4], probably a relation of this governor, restored the theatre at Patara in the same district. In the west of Pisidia too at Comama an inscription[5] of this date commemorates the efforts of Pius to restore the buildings damaged by the earthquake.

The devastation caused by the earthquake was obviously too great to allow of the inhabitants making it good by their own exertions and consequently outside help had to be obtained from all quarters. The Emperor had a special attachment to this district, of part of which he had been proconsul in his earlier days; and, as we have seen, he took the lead in the relief of the wide-spread distress and with great good-will set about the reparation of the damage,—an example which was followed by private individuals[6]. It is interesting to note the efforts which were made at Stratonicea to make good the damage; here one of the inhabitants[7] took the lead and by presents of money and by rebuilding part of the city he earned the lasting gratitude

---

[1] C. I. G. 2718, 2718 c.   [2] C. I. G. 2721.
[3] C. I. G. 4303 h and add. 4303 h¹.   [4] C. I. G. 4283.
[5] Eph. Ep. 5, 1357. [6] Vide supra. C. I. G. 4283. [7] C. I. G. 2721.

of his fellow-townsmen. But he had to fall back on the Emperor, and with an energy not to be expected of his 70 years went on embassy to Rome and laid the case before Antoninus with the result that 240,000 sesterces[1] —roughly £20,000—were granted for the restoration of Stratonicea. To restore the buildings which had been overthrown in Rhodes, Aristides[2] advised the Rhodians to strain every nerve themselves and further to send round to all the Greek cities bidding them equally with the Rhodians to contribute. The Emperor was ready here as elsewhere to make good the damage and in the words of Capitolinus[3] "omnia mirifice instauravit," but this blow seems to have been the last straw among the calamities of Rhodes and she was never able to hold up her head again.

In the third year of his reign the Emperor Antoninus Pius lost his wife[4], Annia Faustina Augusta, the daughter of M. Annius Verus. The character of Faustina has been seriously called in question, but from the scanty evidence at our disposal it seems that no conclusion can be drawn, which shall establish any charge gravely to her discredit. The only suspicion against her is based on Capitolinus[5], who says "de huius uxore multa dicta sunt ob nimiam libertatem et vivendi facultatem, quae iste cum animi dolore conpressit." This charge is on the face of it extremely vague, and at the most asserts that Faustina did not

---

[1] It is uncertain whether this sum is in sesterces or drachmas. Probably the former, as 240,000 dr. = £70,000, and Pius could never have spent so much on a small town, when so many towns required assistance. [2] Arist. (Dind.) 1, 801, 814.
[3] V. P. 9, 1.   [4] V. P. 6, 7.   [5] V. P. 3, 7.

preserve that care for ceremonial and that staid dignity which were expected in an Empress. In another passage Capitolinus[1] shows that she was inclined to use her position in order to advance her personal friends and favourites, and that Antoninus found it necessary to check this unwise propensity.

Of any guilt further than this there is no suspicion. The Emperor was deeply annoyed[2] at the rumours relating to his wife and did his best to silence them effectually; for he was devoted to her and in a letter to Fronto[3] says "mallem me hercule Gyaris cum illa quam sine illa in Palatio vivere." To show his respect for her he allowed the Senate to call her Augusta[4], while he gave the name of Faustinianae[5] to the girls whom he supported by his charitable schemes. It was only when the Senate proposed to go to extreme lengths and to call the months September and October[6] after himself and his wife respectively, that Antoninus objected to the honour. Dedications in honour of Faustina were made throughout Italy, of which one made by the Senate and people of Tibur may be cited as a typical example[7]. Coins also were struck, which prove that harmony existed between the Emperor and his wife and which give the lie to all rumours against Faustina[8]:—

{O = Antoninus Aug. Pius P. P. Tr. P. Cos. III. (Head.)
{R = Concordiae. (Antoninus, *l.* seal of concord. Faustina, *l.* sceptre. Join *r.* hands. Below two figures join hands — probably M. Aurelius and Faustina the younger. In centre an altar.)

[1] *V. P.* 4, 8. [2] *V. P.* 3, 7.
[3] M. Corn. Fronto, *ad Ant. P. et invicem*, 2. [4] *V. P.* 5, 2.
[5] *V. P.* 8, 1. [6] *V. P.* 10, 1. [7] *C. I. L.* xiv. 3580.
[8] Eckhel, 7, 140—143 A.D.; and Cohen, ii. pp. 424 and 425.

At her death in 141 A.D. the Senate conferred divine honours upon Faustina[1], allowed games to be held in her honour and provided for her worship with a temple, priests, and statues of gold and silver; being encouraged to set up statues to her by the fact that Antoninus had already allowed his own image to be exhibited at all the Ludi Circenses.

Thus both publicly and in private Antoninus Pius invited criticism of his relations with his wife, according numerous honours to her, which would attract attention to her. Such conduct is not that of a man desirous to draw a veil over the follies of his wife in order to avoid a public scandal. It rather shows that Antoninus attached no credit to the rumours directed against his wife, and took every means of contradicting the charges by showing to the world that he himself had implicit confidence in her integrity.

Beyond this one fact of the death and canonization of Faustina it is impossible to assign definitely any event of historical importance to the year 141 A.D. Indeed it is practically hopeless in a sketch of the period from the beginning of 140 A.D. to the middle of 144 A.D. to attempt to set down any event as taking place in any particular year, since the historians who treat of Antoninus's reign make practically no attempt to arrange their work in chronological order, while—as it happens—the inscriptions of the period 140—144 A.D. are either politically unimportant or chronologically vague, and finally the coins of these years all bear the

---

[1] *V. P.* 6, 7; Eckhel, 7, *Diva Faustina*; and Cohen, ii. pp. 426 and 427.

date Cos. III with no number attached to the Tribunicia Potestas—though towards the close of 144 A.D. Cos. Des. IIII appears on coins.

Taking the period from the commencement of 140 A.D. to the middle of 144 A.D. as a whole, we find a coin of these years showing that the throne of Armenia had become vacant and that Antoninus Pius appointed a successor to fill the vacancy[1].

{ O = Antoninus Aug. Pius P. P. Tr. P. Cos. III. (Head wreathed.)
R = Rex Armeniis datus. (Emperor with toga crowns an Armenian king.)

Armenia was the half-way house between Rome and Parthia, and—as will be seen subsequently—was involved in difficulties during Antoninus Pius's reign owing to the rôle of buffer-state which she was compelled to play between her two powerful neighbours.

On another frontier Antoninus Pius set up a king over the semi-dependent tribe of the Quadi, who lived to the north of Pannonia on the further side of the Danube. That this event occurred about this time may be seen from a coin[2] quoted by Eckhel:—

{ O = Antoninus Aug. Pius P. P. Tr. P. Cos. III. (Head wreathed.)
R = Rex Quadis datus S.C. (Emperor with toga takes the hand of the king of the Quadi.)

The dependence of the Quadi was always of a doubtful nature; for we find that at the beginning of M. Aurelius's

[1] Eckhel, 7, ad ann. 140—143; and Cohen, 686.
[2] Eckhel, 7, ad ann. 140—143; and Cohen, 687, 688.

reign[1] they refused to confirm the appointment of a king, unless Marcus gave his approval, while by the middle of that Emperor's rule they were active participators in a serious revolt against the Roman power[2].

The whole of the Northern frontier was in a dangerous and threatening condition during Antoninus Pius's reign, though serious outbreak was averted till after his death. The Dacians broke out into insurrection under Pius, the Quadi remained quiet but rose against M. Aurelius, while further to the West the Germans occasioned some trouble, probably between the years 140 and 145 A.D. An inscription[3] found in Rome commemorates the victory of Antoninus over the Germans:—

> Germanos Maurosque domas sub Marte Guitanos[4] (?),
> Antonine tua diceris arte Pius.

Capitolinus[5] too states that Antoninus Pius crushed a revolt of the Germans by means of his legate, while Aristides[6] mentions the complete submission of the Celts, including apparently the Germans under that name.

There is little authority by which the date of the German rising may be fixed, but a milestone[7] with Antoninus Pius Cos. III upon it has been found 30 miles from Cologne on the direct road to Coblenz, and milestones[8] of 139 A.D. have been discovered in the neigh-

---

[1] *V. Marc.* 14, 3.   [2] *V. Marc.* 17, 3; 22, 1; 27, 10.   [3] *C. I. L.* vi. 1208.
[4] ? Quidanos,—from Quiza in Mauretania; cf. *C. I. L.* viii. 9699; ? Aquitanos; ? Britannos.
[5] *V. P.* 5, 4.   [6] Arist. (Dind.) 1, 111.   [7] *C. I. Rh.* 1930.
[8] *C. I. Rh.* 1937, 1965.

bourhood of the town of Trèves. Thus in the early part of Antoninus's reign roads were being built in the Rhine valley, while from 141—143 A.D. a similar work[1] was being carried on in Noricum; and again in Rhaetia during the same period several dedications[2] were made in honour of Antoninus. These facts seem to point to considerable Roman activity on the Northern frontier and especially in Germania during the early part of Antoninus's reign; it is therefore reasonable to suggest the years 140—145 A.D. as probably, but by no means certainly, the period during which the German rebellion occurred—a rising of which nothing is known save that the forces at the disposal of the governor were sufficient to meet the difficulty[3].

Further events of the period 140 A.D. to the middle of 144 A.D. are unimportant and do not call for much attention. On two occasions during this period Antoninus distributed a Congiarium to the populace, but neither of these distributions can be certainly connected with any known occurrence of his reign— assuredly not with the marriage of M. Aurelius and Faustina, which did not take place till 146 A.D.[4]. Coins were struck to commemorate this liberality on the part of the Emperor[5].

{ O = Antoninus Aug. Pius P. P. Tr. P. Cos. III.
{ R = Liberalitas Aug. II. (or III).

[1] *C. I. L.* iii. 5734, 5743.

[2] *C. I. L.* iii. 5906, 5912, 5918 a.   [3] *V. P.* 5, 4.

[4] Eckhel, 7, ad ann. 140—143, connects Lib. II. and Lib. III. with this marriage, but it will be seen below that this marriage clearly took place in 146 A.D.; cf. Cohen, 483—489.

[5] Eckhel, 7, ad ann. 140—143; Cohen, *Ant. P.* 175—177 and 651.

Within the same period another type of coin was struck:—

{Antoninus Aug. Pius P. P. Tr. P. Cos. III. (Head wreathed.)
{Opi Aug. (Woman, r. spear. l. supports her head.)

which seems to point to the fact that the Emperor had now established security throughout his dominions, with the result that plenty followed.

In 143 A.D. Antoninus was engaged in North Italy repairing the Aemilian Way at a distance of 188 miles from Rome[1]. It is seen from inscriptions that within the years 143 and 145 A.D. Antoninus Pius was making great efforts to thoroughly improve the means of communication in Gallia Narbonensis. As early as the year 139 A.D. he restored a road[2] between Aquae Sextiae and Arelate, but it was not till some years afterwards that any serious amount of work was undertaken in the district. The Via Aemilia leading from North Italy through Liguria into Gallia Narbonensis had been repaired in 143 A.D., and this seems to have been a preparatory step to setting in order the roads of Gallia Narbonensis. A great number of inscriptions are found referring to the building or restoration of the roads here by Antoninus, which, bearing for the most part the date Tr. P. VII, Cos. IV, must in consequence be assigned to the period between Jan. 1 and Feb. 25, 145 A.D.[3]

The roads which were built or restored during this period or the preceding year were:—

---

[1] Orelli, *Inscr.* 136.   [2] *C. I. L.* xii. 5477.
[3] The inscriptions are on milestones, which would be set up when the road was completed.

REIGN OF ANTONINUS PIUS TILL 148 A.D.

(1) From Forum Iulii to Reii[1].
(2) From Forum Iulii to Aquae Sextiae[2].
(3) From Brigantio to Arelate[3].
(4) From Glanum to Ugernum[4].
(5) From Noviodunum to Genavum[5].
(6) From Lugdunum to Arelate, along the left bank of the Rhone[6].
(7) From Alba to Burgum, on the right bank of the Rhone[7].
(8) From Alba to Ucetia[8].
(9) From Arelate to Nemausus[9].
(10) From Nemausus to Narbo[10].

It is probable that in most of these cases Antoninus Pius did nothing more than restore the existing roads, with perhaps some slight improvements and additions in certain directions; for Gallia Narbonensis was certainly fairly well supplied with roads before this time[11]. Nor can the main object of the roads have been military, since the troops of Rome were under the Emperors kept upon the frontiers of the Empire and seldom appeared in a thoroughly quiet district like Gallia Narbonensis. The object of the road-making of Antoninus Pius in this district can only have been the developement and extension of commerce in the S.E. of Gaul. Roads were built or restored to supplement the river Rhone as a trade-route from the interior; others were

---

[1] *C. I. L.* xii. 5453. [2] *C. I. L.* xii. 5458, 5464.
[3] *C. I. L.* xii. 5499. [4] *C. I. L.* xii. 5501. [5] 5533.
[6] 5541, 5544, 5551 (not finished till 147 A.D.).
[7] *C. I. L.* xii. 5564—5570. [8] 5573—5583.
[9] 5603, 5604, 5616. [10] 5625, 5626, 5629, 5639.
[11] *C. I. L.* xii. Viae publicae.

built or restored between provincial towns to increase the facilities of exchange; while from Arelate, Massilia or Narbo on the south coast the goods, which had come by road or river from the interior of the country, could be carried by sea to all parts of the Empire or transported on land by the Via Domitia and the Via Aurelia to Rome. That Antoninus showed more activity in road-making in Gallia Narbonensis than in any other part of his Empire, is due to the fact that he himself was by origin a native of the district[1] and, though born and bred in Italy, still retained a feeling of sympathy with the district from which his ancestors had sprung.

Towards the end of 144 A.D. coins[2] were struck bearing the title Cos. III, Des. IIII, and on some of them there is a figure of Hygeia:—

{O = Antoninus Aug. Pius P. P. Tr. P. Cos. III. (Head.)
{R = Des. IIII. (Hygeia standing.)

Now Pausanias[3] mentions that Antoninus Pius built various temples at or near Epidaurus, and showed great liberality to the temple-hospital there. Pausanias states that Antoninus set up among other buildings a temple to Hygeia, Aesculapius and Apollo; it is perhaps not too venturesome to suppose that the coins referring to Hygeia and the temple at Epidaurus belong to the same date.

For the year 145 A.D. the Emperor was himself consul[4] for the fourth time—the last occasion on which he assumed this office—and he had for his colleague M. Aurelius Cos. II. During the course of this year

[1] V. P. 1, 1.   [2] Eckhel, 7, ad ann. 144.   [3] Paus. 2. 27, 7.
[4] C. I. L. vi. 2085; Eckhel, 7, M. Aur. Ant., 145 A.D.

Lucius, the other adopted son of Antoninus Pius, assumed the Toga Virilis. From Capitolinus's life of Verus[1] it appears that this Lucius Verus was adopted at the close of his seventh year, and that he lived as "privatus" for 23 years in the Imperial house. Now it has been shown that L. Verus was adopted in 138 A.D., while the reign of Antoninus Pius lasted for 23 years. Accordingly it is clear that L. Verus was 7 years old in 138 A.D. or 30 years old in 161 A.D., i.e. he was born in 131 A.D. Again, from various sources[2] it is clear that the Toga Virilis was assumed in the course of the 15th year; and consequently L. Verus's assumption of the Toga Virilis may be certainly set down for the year 145 A.D.

Coupled with this event were the dedication by Antoninus of a temple to Hadrian and the distribution of a Congiarium[3]. Capitolinus[4] in his life of Pius mentions the temple of Hadrian—"honori patris dicatum"—as one of the works of Pius. It appears, however, from coins[5] not to have been completed till 151 A.D.; the statement that a Congiarium was distributed at the same time is perhaps confirmed by coins, which Eckhel assigns to this year, but which might equally well belong to 146 A.D.[6]:—

{ O = Antoninus Aug. Pius P. P. (Head wreathed.)
{ R = Lib. IIII. Cos. IIII. (Woman standing, r. tessera frumentaria; l. cornucopiae.)

[1] *V. Veri*, 2, 10 and 11.
[2] *V. Marc.* 5, 5; cf. Festus, s.v. Vesticeps; cf. Willems, *D. P. R.* 68, n. 7.
[3] *V. Veri*, 3, 1.   [4] *V. P.* 8, 2.   [5] Eckhel, 7, ad ann. 151.
[6] Eckhel, 7, ad ann. 145; Cohen, *Ant. P.* 188—193, 512, 652, 661—663.

58 THE REIGN OF ANTONINUS PIUS.

On one of the coins quoted by Cohen—No. 512—the figure of the Praef. Praet. occurs pointing to the fact that the Praetorians shared in the distribution, while in some examples[1] a "labarum" or military standard takes the place of the "tessera frumentaria" or corn-ticket, showing that Antoninus in the words of Capitolinus[2] "congiarium populo dedit, militibus donativum addidit."

In the year 146 A.D. M. Aurelius married Faustina, the daughter of Antoninus Pius[3]. The date of the marriage is fixed by the fact that Capitolinus[4] puts it after Marcus's second consulship (145 A.D.), while he received the *Tribunicia potestas* on the birth of his first child. Marcus was in the 15th year of his Tr. Pot. when he became Emperor[5]; and accordingly he received the Tr. Pot. first in 147 A.D., i.e. he was married in 146 A.D. A coin[6] of Ephesus confirms this date:—

{O = ΟΥΗΡΟC ΚΑΙCΑΡ ΦΑΥCΤΕΙΝΑ CΕ. (Heads of Marcus and
{R = ΕΠΙ ΚΛ. ΙΟΥΛΙΑΝΟΥ ΕΦΕCΙΩΝ. Faustina.)

The coin commemorating the marriage of Marcus and Faustina was struck in the proconsulship of Julianus; Julianus was, according to Waddington[7], proconsul of Asia from the spring of 145 A.D. to the spring of 146 A.D.; consequently the marriage took place before the summer of 146 A.D. Capitolinus[8] says that Antoninus celebrated this marriage of his adopted son to Faustina by a present

---

[1] Eckhel, 7, ad ann. 145.   [2] *V. P.* 8, 1.   [3] *V. P.* 10, 2.
[4] *V. Marc.* 6, 6.   [5] Eckhel, *M. Aur. Ant.* ad ann. 161.
[6] Mionnet, *Ionia*, No. 321.
[7] Wadd. *mémoire sur la vie d'Aristide* (*Mém. de l'Acad.* 1867, p. 211).
[8] *V. P.* 10, 2.

to the soldiers—" usque ad donativum militum celeberrimas fecit." Now, from the coins quoted by Eckhel and Cohen, Liberalitas III must be put within the years 140—143 A.D. and Liberalitas V in 148 A.D.[1] But between these two dates there were two occasions on which Antoninus Pius made presents to the people or to the soldiers—the taking of the Toga Virilis by L. Verus and the marriage of Marcus Aurelius. However, it is only stated that the soldiers received a donation on the second occasion; and consequently it is perhaps better to agree with Eckhel in fixing the fourth Congiarium (Lib. III) to the year 145 A.D., and to suppose that on the occasion of the marriage of Marcus Aurelius in the beginning of 146 A.D. only the soldiers received presents, rather than to imagine that one Congiarium is completely ignored by coins.

In the year 147 A.D. M. Aurelius had his first child born to him[2]—a daughter—and the occasion was honoured by the admission of Marcus to a much fuller share of Imperial power than he had previously held. He now received the Tribunicia Potestas, Proconsulare Imperium, outside the City, and the "ius quintae relationis," or the right to submit five subjects to the Senate before the ordinary magistrates could bring any business forward[3]. The early Emperors had—when unable to be present—sent a written document entitled "oratio" or "litterae," which took precedence over all other matters in the Senate. The procedure, when the Emperor was present, was substantially the same, and

---

[1] Eckhel, 7, ad ann. 140—148; Cohen, 175—177 and 651; and Eckhel, 7, ad ann. 148; Cohen, 182, 194, 195.
[2] V. Marc. 6, 6.   [3] Willems, D. P. R. 437.

subsequent Emperors claimed the right to bring up three, four and five subjects for discussion before any other business was taken. Thus Antoninus Pius now conferred on Marcus a dignity which had been the recognized accompaniment of full Imperial power, while the conferring of Tribunicia Potestas and Proconsulare Imperium made Marcus nominally the equal of the Emperor, since these two powers were the foundations respectively of the Emperor's political and military power. At the same time Faustina, the wife of Marcus, received the title of Augusta[1].

But in spite of the honours thus heaped upon Marcus and his wife, there was never—as we shall see subsequently in a more systematic examination of Marcus's position—any question of equality of power between Antoninus Pius and M. Aurelius. Antoninus's hand was always ready to guide and to direct, and his promotion of Marcus sprang from a desire to train him in the duties of empire and to accustom him to its responsibilities, rather than from a wish to make him Emperor before his time. Indeed on coins, which bear the name of M. Aurelius, the titles "Consul," "Trib. Pot.," "Caesar," are found belonging to the period while Antoninus Pius was still alive; but not till 161 A.D. does the Imperial title "Imperator Caesar...Augustus" appear.

The year 147 A.D. is also notable as being the 900th anniversary of the foundation of the City, and Antoninus celebrated this occasion with all due splendour and magnificence[2]. What particular form the

[1] Cf. Eckhel, 7, ad ann. 147 A.D. (Faust. Iunior); and Cohen, ii. p. 442; cf. *C. I. L.* ii. 4097, 3391.
[2] S. Aur. Victor, *De Caess.* 15.

celebration took is not known, but Antoninus's "insignis erga caerimonias publicas cura et religio"[1] would certainly not allow him to leave anything undone which might add to the glory of the occasion. Coins bearing mythological devices[2] were struck at various dates throughout this reign, and many of the scenes depicted are connected with the origin of Rome, e.g. the story of Hercules and Cacus[3], the escape of Aeneas with his father and son from Troy, the landing of Aeneas in Italy, Mars and Rhea—a coin which represents Mars hanging in the air over the sleeping Rhea[4],—the she-wolf suckling the twins Romulus and Remus. It may fairly be assumed that these coins were struck in honour of the 900th anniversary of the City. Pausanias[5] says that Pius's commemoration of the 900th anniversary took a more practical form, since he raised the Arcadian village of Pallantium—the traditional home of Evander—to the rank of a free town, granting it exemption from taxation, because it was from here that Evander set forth to colonize the Palatine Hill at Rome.

The following year, 148 A.D., completed the first 10 years of Antoninus's reign: he had commenced his rule on July 10th, 138 A.D., and it was accordingly on July 10th, 148 A.D., that the 10 years' space was ended, and coins[6] were struck during the year commemorative of this fact:—

{ Antoninus Aug. Pius P. P. Tr. P. XI. (Head wreathed.)
{ Primi Decennales. (Wreath of oak-leaves round the words.)

[1] *C. I. L.* vi. 1001. [2] Eckhel, 7, *Pius's Mythological Coins*.
[3] Cf. Ov. *Ff.* i. 550—580. [4] Cf. Juv. xi. 107, "Pendentisque dei."
[5] Paus. 8, 43. [6] Eckhel, 7, ad ann. 148.

It appears that vows had been taken at the commencement of the reign of Antoninus to be discharged if the Emperor lived and reigned for 10 years. The vows were taken both officially and privately; for a coin shows the Emperor—as representative of the state—sacrificing to the gods in an official capacity[1]:—

{Antoninus Aug. Pius P. P. Tr. P. xi. (Head wreathed.)
{Vot. Cos. iiii. (Emperor sacrificing at a tripod.)

Similarly new vows were officially taken for the succeeding 10 years and the fact was commemorated on coins[2]:—

Vota Suscepta x. Cos. iiii.

Private vows are recorded on a number of inscriptions, which state that individuals and corporate bodies throughout the Empire paid gladly their vows "pro salute Pii." Most of these inscriptions are without any definite date, but their character makes it clear that they must be set down either to 148 A.D. or to 158 A.D. Examples are found in all parts of the Empire —at Puteoli[3], Verona[4], Thibilis in Numidia[5], Uxellodunum (Maryport) in Britain[6], Troesmis in Moesia[7], near Cologne[8], and at many other places.

The Decennial vows were probably a reminiscence of the custom of Augustus, who nominally held his power for 10 years only and nominally laid it down at the end of that period, receiving it again by a new mandate for a new period of 10 years[9]. Subsequent Emperors without going through the farce of laying

---

[1] Eckhel, 7, ad ann. 148.   [2] Eckhel, 7, ad ann. 148.
[3] C. I. L. x. 1562.   [4] C. I. L. v. 3258.   [5] C. I. L. viii. 5523.
[6] C. I. L. vii. 400.   [7] C. I. L. iii. 6162—6168.   [8] C. I. Rh. 305.
[9] Cf. Dio Cass. liii. 16; liv. 12; lviii. 24; lxxvi. 1.

REIGN OF ANTONINUS PIUS TILL 148 A.D.

down their power yet celebrated their tenth year of rule by the giving of games and festivals[1]. There is no account of any games under Antoninus which can be put down definitely for 148 A.D., but it is known that he gave shows on several occasions[2], and there is no reason to doubt that he followed the custom of his predecessors and celebrated games now. Coins[3] of 149 A.D. contain references to shows given by Antoninus, in which apparently lions and elephants were among the beasts exhibited:—

{ Antoninus Aug. Pius P. P. Tr. P. XII. Cos. IIII. (Head with crown.)
Munificentia. (Lion walking.)

{ Antoninus Aug. Pius P. P. Tr. P. XII. (Head wreathed.)
Munificentia. Aug. Cos. IIII. s.c. (Elephant with breastplate.)

The word "Munificentia" can hardly refer to anything but the "Edita Munera" mentioned by Capitolinus[4], while the elephant with breastplate[5] appeared on coins struck for the games of the Emperor Titus. It is certain then that these coins refer to games, and very probably to the decennial games, which may have been held over for a few months until the beginning of 149 A.D.

The only other point of interest of this year, 148 A.D., is that Antoninus now gave his fifth Congiarium and coins were struck to commemorate the fact[6]:—

{ Antoninus Aug. Pius P. P. Tr. P. XI. (Head wreathed.)
Lib. v. Cos. IIII. (Liberality standing.)

---

[1] Willems, *D. P. R.* 409, n. 8; Eckhel, 8, p. 475.
[2] *V. P.* 10, 9.   [3] Eckhel, 7, ad ann. 149 A.D.; and Cohen, 562—566.
[4] *V. P.* 10, 9.   [5] Eckhel, 7, ad ann. 149 A.D.
[6] Eckhel, 7, ad ann. 148 A.D.; Cohen, 182, 194, 195.

Thus ended the first period of 10 years—or rather 10 years and 6 months—during which Antoninus stood at the helm of the Roman state. It was a period marked by few events of importance, and the only disturbances of its otherwise unruffled calm were the outbreaks in Britain and in Germany and the calamitous earthquake in Asia Minor. Yet "happy the nation that has no history," and prosperous the years whose records are vague. The quiet of these 10 years was due to the fact that general contentment existed throughout the Empire, while the Emperor by his decisive action in dealing with rebellions—as he dealt with the rebellion in Britain—held out no encouragement to other turbulent spirits to presume on the age and gentleness of Antoninus. It would seem indeed that underneath the quiet and calm of these years a good and vigorous administration was at work to secure this peaceful condition of affairs; and it would be a complete mistake to imagine that the Emperor Antoninus Pius with the advance of years had become senile and weak, too feeble to resent any insult to the majesty of Rome and of the Emperor, content only to sleep away in ignoble apathy the declining years of his life.

CHAPTER IV.

REIGN OF ANTONINUS PIUS, 148—161 A.D.

THE first period of ten years in Antoninus's reign had been marked by the quiet prosperity and peaceful progress which are the chief blessings of good government. Nor was the course of the years 149—151 A.D. different in character from that of the preceding ten years, if we may draw any inference from the absence of information with regard to them. The coins of the period are of little assistance, but, as far as they go, they tend to support the theory of quiet prosperity at that time. In 149 A.D. a coin[1] was struck of the following type:—

{ Antoninus Aug. Pius P. P. Tr. P. XII. (Head.)
{ Temporum Felicitas. Cos. IIII. (Two cornucopiae, on each of which is the head of a child.)

This undoubtedly shows the prosperity of the times, but it is less certain what the meaning of the two children's heads may be. Eckhel conjectures that they refer to the birth of twin children of M. Aurelius, and this is a very possible supposition, which in default of any further evidence may be regarded as true.

[1] Eckhel, 7, ad ann. 149 A.D.

Then again in 151 A.D. another type of coin was struck[1]:—

{ Antoninus Aug. Pius P. P. Tr. P. XIIII.
 Laetitia. Cos. IIII.

which points to continued prosperity both by its inscription and also by the device, which in some examples shows two figures in togas holding ears of corn and a globe, in others a woman standing with ears of corn and an apple in her hand, while a boy clings to her waist.

In 149 A.D. Antoninus Pius exhibited the games, which have already been mentioned as forming part of the celebration of his 10th year of Empire[2]. But after that there is no record of any event till the year 151 A.D., when he bestowed the sixth Congiarium on the people in the 14th year of his Tribunicia Potestas[3].

In the same year a coin[4] was struck, which bears the ordinary inscription of the Emperor's name and titles with the year of his Tribunicia Potestas, while on the reverse is a representation of a temple with eight pillars, in which sit two figures holding spears. Eckhel is probably correct in supposing that the two figures represent Hadrian and Sabina, and in identifying the temple with the Templum Hadriani, included by Capitolinus[5] among the works of Antoninus Pius. He omits however to notice that the dedication of the temple is placed by Capitolinus[6] in 145 A.D. Perhaps it may have been finished in its original form in 145 A.D., while

---

[1] Eckhel, 7, ad ann. 151 A.D.   [2] v. supra, chap. III.
[3] Cohen, *Ant. P.* 196 and 197.   [4] Eckhel, 7, ad ann. 151 A.D.
[5] *V. P.* 8, 2.   [6] *V. Veri*, 3, 1.

in 151 A.D. an extra chapel or aisle may have been added for the worship of Diva Faustina.

It was probably at the close of 151 A.D. or the commencement of 152 A.D. that a second disastrous earthquake occurred, extending, as has been seen in the account of the former earthquake, over most of the north-western corner of Asia Minor and laying Mitylene, Smyrna, Ephesus, Cyzicus and the cities of Bithynia in ruins. With regard to the date of this earthquake Aristides[1] places it in the proconsulship of Albus, and Waddington states that L. Antonius Albus was proconsul of Asia at some time between the years 147 A.D. and 152 A.D.[2] Again, the Rescript *ad Commune Asiae* quoted by Eusebius[3] as an order of Antoninus Pius refers to an earthquake, which had just happened in Asia Minor. The difficulty with regard to this rescript is that, whereas Eusebius undoubtedly assigns it to Antoninus Pius, yet, when he gives the text of it, he makes M. Aurelius the author of the ordinance. It is probable that Eusebius has confused the name of the two Emperors and that Antoninus Pius should be regarded as the author of the document, if it is to be considered genuine[4]. If that be so, the rescript must be assigned to the year 152 A.D. owing to the presence of the date Tr. Pot. XV after the Emperor's name, and

[1] Arist. (Dind.) 1, 497.

[2] Waddington, *sur la vie d'Aristide* (*Mém. de l'Acad.* 1867, p. 245).

[3] Euseb. *H. E.* iv. 13.

[4] The genuineness of the rescript does not alter its value as evidence concerning the earthquake. The author of a forgery would be careful of his historical references. Cf. Ramsay (*Church in Rom. Empire*, p. 332, n. 5), who regards it as a forgery. Mommsen and Lightfoot believe that it belongs to the year 158 A.D.

68   THE REIGN OF ANTONINUS PIUS.

the earthquake referred to as having just happened can then be fixed to the year 151 A.D. or the beginning of 152 A.D.

Aristides[1] states that Mitylene was now almost completely destroyed, the whole town being reduced to ruins, while Smyrna and Ephesus were thrown into confusion and terror and the whole configuration of the country was changed, so violent was the earthquake. Zonaras[2] states that Bithynia and the Hellespont suffered especially from this earthquake; for many cities, and among them Cyzicus, were laid in ruins. At Cyzicus the famous temple was overthrown, whose pillars are said to have been 4 fathoms thick, 50 cubits high and made of one stone, εἴ τῳ ταῦτα μὴ ἄπιστα δόξαιεν, while the rest of the temple was on the same scale.

Foremost in the task of repairing the damage caused by this earthquake was M. Aurelius, who from his friendship with Fronto and other literary men felt an interest in these cities, which had been the homes of literature in the past and which even now numbered literary men among their inhabitants. Polemon, the powerful but sour orator, was living at Smyrna[3], and he had had considerable influence with Trajan and Hadrian; while Favorinus[4], the rival of Polemon and friend of Fronto and Herodes Atticus, was living at Ephesus, honoured by his fellow-townsmen. Accordingly we find from a coin[5] that M. Aurelius did what was in

[1] Arist. (Dind.) 1, 497.   [2] Zonaras, xii. P. 1, 593 c.; V. P. 9, 1.
[3] Philostr. v. Sophist. 1, 25, pp. 531, 532.
[4] Philostr. v. Sophist. 1, 8, pp. 489—491.
[5] Mionnet, iii. No. 1296.

his power to restore Smyrna to its former condition, and Philostratus[1] says that it was Aristides who induced him to do so. At Nicomedia in Bithynia, the home of the now aged Arrian, and again at Ephesus, Antoninus Pius built baths[2], and these were probably part of the work of restoration. Nothing more however is known of the details of the restoration, but we may conclude that it was satisfactorily carried out, for Pausanias[3] states that Antoninus Pius made many presents of money to the Greeks and barbarians, and erected many buildings in Ionia.

About the same time as the earthquake in Northwest Asia Minor affairs in Africa, which had long been a source of anxiety to Rome, came to a crisis and demanded vigorous military action. The north coast of Africa, from Carthage to the Atlantic Ocean, with its narrow strip of cultivated land 100 miles in breadth lying between the Mediterranean on the North and the desert on the South, has always been the home of marauders and brigands of all descriptions, owing both to its sparse population and to the mountainous character of the district. Under the rule of Antoninus Pius this brigandage seems to have become unbearable. Fronto[4] refers to the insecurity of the roads in Mauretania and to the skill of Iulius Senex in dealing with the intolerable plague of robbers. And again in an inscription[5] found in the district south of Lambaesis, attention is drawn to the danger of travelling in that district, where lay the Saltus Aurasius—a group of

---

[1] Philostr. v. Sophist. 582.   [2] Malala (ed. Bonn) xi. 281.
[3] Paus. 8, 43.   [4] Fronto, *ad Ant. P.* 3, 8.
[5] *C. I. L.* viii. 2728 = Wilmanns, 785.

hills affording an almost impregnable refuge to the outcasts and criminals of the neighbourhood. It seems probable that various acts of brigandage had been committed during Antoninus Pius's reign, before 145 A.D., in the neighbourhood of Lambaesis in Numidia. At that date an attempt was made to open up the Saltus Aurasius by building a road across the hills behind Lambaesis[1]. The work was performed by Vexillarii of Legio VI (Ferrata) acting under the direction of Prastina Messalinus, the governor of Numidia, who became consul in 147 A.D.[2] At the same time or a little later an aqueduct was commenced[3], which was intended to supply Lambaesis with water from the hills. But the progress of this work was slow, from the danger of working in the presence of bandits, and the aqueduct was still unfinished in 152 A.D., although Legio III (Augusta) was stationed at Lambaesis for the protection of the district[4].

Yet in spite of the fact that the bandits still held out in the wilder parts of the Saltus Aurasius, it seems that the province of Numidia had been practically freed from its pest by the year 150 A.D. The brigands had in fact been gradually driven westwards and had finally taken refuge in Mauretania, where in company with the nomadic tribes of the hill country of Mt. Atlas they organized a vigorous resistance to the Roman forces. This conduct compelled the Romans to take active and decisive measures, and instead of merely maintaining order in the district to undertake a real war—a change in the aspect of affairs, which may be

[1] C. I. L. viii. 10230.
[2] C. I. L. ix. 1573.
[3] C. I. L. viii. 2728.
[4] C. I. L. viii. 2536—2541.

dated fairly nearly by means of two inscriptions found in the district. From the first of these it appears that T. Varius Clemens[1], who in the course of a long career was Imperial procurator of the provinces of Raetia, Mauretania Caesariensis, Lusitania, Cilicia, Belgica, Germania Inferior and Superior, and held various military appointments throughout the Empire, was appointed "Praefectus auxiliariorum tempore expeditionis in Tingitanam ex Hispania missorum." From the second inscription[2] we find the same T. Varius Clemens complaining to the governor of Numidia, Valerius Etruscus, about the insecurity of travelling in the neighbourhood of Lambaesis owing to "latrones." Now Valerius Etruscus was governor of Numidia in 152 A.D.[3], and it may therefore be reasonably conjectured that about this time Clemens was sent from Lusitania, of which district he was procurator, at the head of a Spanish contingent, to cooperate with the troops in Africa in making a punitive expedition into the uplands of Tingitana, the western part of Mauretania. After the war in Tingitana was concluded—as far as such guerilla warfare can be concluded—Clemens seems to have gone east into Numidia, and there to have fallen in with brigands near Lambaesis. It is probable that he now stayed somewhile in Africa and his procuratorship of Mauretania may have fallen at this date.

Lacour-Gayet[4] puts the Moorish war of Antoninus

---

[1] Wilmanns, 1260, a, b, and c. [2] *C. I. L.* viii. 2728.
[3] *C. I. L.* viii. 2543; Eph. Ep. 5, 686.
[4] Lacour-Gayet, *Ant. P.* p. 142. Cagnat (*L'armée Romain d'Afrique*, pp. 41—44) puts the war between 144 and 149 A.D.

72   THE REIGN OF ANTONINUS PIUS.

Pius before the year 143 A.D., reckoning that the road across the Saltus Aurasius[1]—made in 145 A.D.—was commenced after the war was finished, and that Pausanias[2] in giving his account of the Moorish war before that of the British war of Antoninus is following the chronological order of events. But with a writer of a thoroughly discursive character like Pausanias, the argument from arrangement is of absolutely no value, nor can any inference be drawn from the order of the titles of T. Varius Clemens[3], as to when he was procurator of Mauretania. The theory that the eastern part of the district was first cleared of robbers and that they were gradually pushed westward, coincides with what is known of the condition of the Northern coast-line of Africa, where Numidia was generally quite peaceful, where Mauretania Caesariensis had only been conquered in 42 A.D., and where the west of Mauretania was still only nominally subject to the Romans. Lacour-Gayet's view on the other hand requires us to suppose that the turbulent tribes of the West were first subdued, and that the generally peaceful Eastern district was the last to be quieted. We must therefore reject Lacour-Gayet's theory and his date, and accept the year 152 as the probable date of the Moorish rising.

Capitolinus[4] dismisses the Moorish war with the brief remark that Pius compelled the Mauri to sue for peace. Pausanias[5] devotes a little more space to it and regards the war as a struggle of considerable importance, forced upon the Emperor by the action of the independent tribe of the Mauri. He is technically wrong

[1] C. I. L. viii. 10230.   [2] Paus. 8, 43, 3 and 4.
[3] Wilmanns, 1260.   [4] V. P. 5, 4.   [5] Paus. 8, 43, 3.

in saying that the Mauri were independent, for the eastern part of Mauretania, i.e. Mauretania Caesariensis, became a Roman province in 42 A.D., while even over the western district of Tingitana the Romans had a nominal control. But the actual extent of Roman authority over a warlike and nomadic people such as the Mauri must have been vague and variable. Pausanias goes on to say that "these Mauri were nomadic and more warlike than the Scythians, for they fought not from waggons, but themselves and their wives riding on horseback. Yet Pius drove them from all their land to the extremities of Mt. Atlas and the shores of the Atlantic." These words of Pausanias exactly confirm the theory that the eastern district was first cleared, and that the brigands and the Mauri were gradually pushed westward to the shores of the Atlantic. And if this theory can be regarded as established, there is no room for doubting that 152 A.D. is the approximate date of the military action of the Romans in Tingitana.

The disturbances in Mauretania had scarcely been quieted, when attention was directed to the eastern end of the north coast of Africa by a revolt of the Egyptians. Capitolinus[1] mentions the Egyptians as in rebellion during Pius's reign, and Aristides[2] alludes briefly to "some mad attempt of the people living round the shores of the Red Sea." The exact date and nature of the outbreak cannot be definitely stated, but we hear from Malala[3] that Dinarchus was prefect of Egypt at the time, having succeeded Avidius Helio-

[1] *V. P.* 5, 4.   [2] Arist. (Dind.) 1, 351.
[3] Malala (Bonn) xi. p. 280.

dorus, who remained in office till about 148 A.D.[1] Accordingly, 148 A.D. is the earliest date at which the outbreak can have taken place. Again, from Malala[2] we learn that Antoninus Pius, as soon as the outbreak in Egypt had been finally subdued, set about erecting some buildings at Alexandria and then went on to Syria. Now Waddington[3] shows that this visit of Antoninus to Syria is not later than 154 or 155 A.D., so that allowing for the time spent on the building operations in Alexandria, the conclusion of the war must be placed within a few months of the close of the year 153 A.D. But it must be remembered at the same time that Aristides and Malala cannot be considered good authorities, when the question is one of determining the exact date of any occurrence; and Waddington fixes the date of Antoninus Pius's visit to Syria merely from a statement made by Aristides as to the progress of an illness, from which he himself was suffering at the time. It would then perhaps be safer not to attempt to fix the date of the Egyptian revolt at all, but if a date is to be fixed, 153 A.D. may be considered to be the most likely year for the outbreak.

The revolt does not seem to have been particularly serious, but its gravity was enhanced by the fact that Rome obtained so great a proportion of her corn from Egypt. The population of a large trading town like Alexandria was necessarily very composite, and faction-

[1] *C. I. G.* 4955; cf. Letronne, *Inscr. Egypt.* 1, 133.
[2] Malala (Bonn) xi. p. 280.
[3] Arist. (Dind.) 1, 453—454. Waddington, *sur la vie d'Aristide* (*Mém. de l'Acad.* 1867, pp. 232—234).

fights, developing not seldom into resistance to the Roman authority, were common enough in the city. Yet if the words of Aristides[1] are to be pressed, the revolt arose on the shores of the Red Sea, i.e. in Upper Egypt. Malala[2] supports the statement of Aristides in assigning Upper Egypt as the scene of the revolt, for he says that Antoninus Pius finished the war and then returned to Alexandria. He adds that Dinarchus, the prefect of Egypt, was murdered by the rebels. Inscriptions prove that within a few years of the outbreak there was a considerable military force in Upper Egypt, consisting of Legio II (Traiana $\mathit{l\sigma\chi\upsilon\rho\grave{a}}$) and a cohort of Ituraeans, while a Turma of Hispani was quartered in Nubia[3]. It might have been thought that this force was amply sufficient to cope with any local disturbance, yet Malala[4] definitely states that the Emperor himself came to Egypt to subdue the rebels. Now Capitolinus[5] certainly implies that Antoninus Pius stayed in or near Rome during the whole length of his reign; though the phrase "nullas expeditiones obiit" may not explicitly deny that he went on any military enterprises, but may merely refer to a change from Hadrian's system of touring through the provinces. On the other hand, Malala[6] and Aristides[7] assert that Antoninus Pius visited Syria as well as Egypt. And since Capitolinus leaves some room for doubt, we must accept the testimony of these two writers, and conclude that the Emperor did visit Egypt in person, possibly in consequence of the traditional policy of Roman Emperors, who were

---

[1] Arist. (Dind.) 1, 351.   [2] Malala, xi. p. 280.
[3] C. I. G. 4766, 5047, 5050.   [4] Malala, l. c.   [5] V. P. 7, 11.
[6] Malala, l. c.   [7] Arist. (Dind.) 1, 453, 454.

afraid to admit any Roman of rank and importance save themselves into Egypt. The suppression of the revolt seems to have been a matter of little difficulty[1], and Antoninus Pius soon returned to Alexandria, in which city he set up the Gates of the Sun and of the Moon, and laid out a racecourse[2]. The country being then thoroughly peaceful he set sail for Antioch.

In the year 154 A.D., about the time of his departure from Alexandria for Antioch, Antoninus Pius caused to be distributed at Rome during his absence his seventh Congiarium. This distribution is recorded on the coins[3] of the year:—

{ Antoninus Aug. Pius P. P. Tr. P. XVII. (Head.)
{ Liberalitas VII. Cos. IIII. (i, Liberality standing.
     or ii, Emperor standing. *r.* Tessera
       frumentaria. *l.* Roll of those
       qualified to receive.
     or iii, Woman pouring corn from
       cornucopiae.)

Arriving in Antioch in the year 154 A.D., Antoninus Pius found a state of affairs which needed his careful management. Trajan had conquered the Parthians, but his success was purely military, and consequently vigorous military action and a constant display of physical force were needed to keep in check the district which had been won. Hadrian, however, had adopted a different policy from his predecessor's, treating with kindness and consideration the conquered nations, while he practically left the Parthians to themselves and hoped that the nominal supremacy of Rome would be enough to

---

[1] *V. P.* 5, 4.   [2] Malala, xi. 280.
[3] Eckhel, 7, ad ann. 154 A.D.; Cohen, *Ant. P.* 183—187.

keep them quiet. But this was not the right way to ensure the fidelity of those who were only waiting for evidences of weakness in order to throw off a precarious yoke, and Hadrian reaped the reward of his misunderstood leniency in the Jewish outbreak of 132 A.D. Nor was it long before the Parthians began to make trial of the temper of the Roman Emperor. At the commencement of the reign of Antoninus Pius the king of Parthia sent to solicit from the Emperor the restoration of the Royal throne, which Trajan had taken from the Parthians[1], accompanying his request with the presentation of "aurum coronarium" to the Emperor[2]. This request was met, however, by a definite refusal; whereupon the Parthian king made another move, and attacked the neighbouring kingdom of Armenia[3], over which Antoninus Pius had set up a king between the years 140 and 143 A.D.[4] Yet he was not prepared to come into actual conflict with the Roman legions, and on receiving an order from Antoninus to withdraw into his own dominions he complied with the command[5]. But though quiet for awhile, he was still ready to seize any opportunity that offered itself of rising against Rome.

The movements of the Parthians were not, however, the only cause for anxiety in the East. Abgarus[6], of Edessa[7], had attacked one of the neighbouring kinglets, and was only restrained from proceeding to further lengths by the admonition of Antoninus Pius.

---

[1] *V. P.* 9, 7. [2] Eckhel, 7, ad ann. 139 A.D. [3] *V. P.* 9, 6.
[4] Eckhel, 7, ad ann. 140—143 A.D. [5] *V. P.* 9, 6.
[6] *V. P.* 9, 6.
[7] Lacour-Gayet, *Ant. P.* p. 151; cf. Chron. Edess. § viii.

Then again Capitolinus[1] refers to a revolt of the Jews, which was put down during Antoninus's reign, and there are three references in Justin Martyr's *Dialogus cum Tryphone*[2] to a war just finished in Judaea and to some severe punishment inflicted on the Jews in consequence. Now this dialogue was written as an addition or explanation to the first Apology[3], and this Apology gives its own date as 150 A.D.[4] This date may, of course, be only approximate, but it seems at least probable that the Apology cannot have been written before 138 A.D., while the *Dialogus cum Tryphone* is generally assigned approximately to the year 150 A.D.[5] There seems then no doubt that there was a Jewish rebellion in Antoninus Pius's reign as well as in Hadrian's, and that both Capitolinus and Justin Martyr refer to the same outbreak.

Again, during Antoninus's reign, the Alani occasioned a considerable amount of trouble by a variety of movements[6], of which nothing is known, but which Antoninus had always to be on the alert to frustrate. They were an important tribe on the northern slopes of the Caucasus, whose geographical position rendered them dangerous neighbours and at the same time afforded them protection from any attack. Against such foes as this it was necessary to protect the numerous semi-dependent states which lay along the Eastern frontier

---

[1] *V. P.* 5, 5.   [2] Just. Mart. *Dial. c. Tryph.* 217 c. 227, 234 c.
[3] Cf. Otto, Prolegomena to Just. Martyr. 1, lxxxiv.   [4] 1, 46.
[5] Cf. the late Prof. Hort on the date (*Journal of Class. and Sacr. Philol.* iii. 1856, p. 155—193); cf. Lightfoot, *Apost. Fathers*, ii. 1, 462, 518. Cf. Ramsay (*Church in R. E.*, p. 320), who puts the First Apology about 140 A.D.   [6] *V. P.* 5, 5.

of the Roman Empire, and an inscription[1] found at Venice, referring to a soldier who had served against the Alani, may contain a reference to Antoninus Pius's wars with this tribe. Arrian[2] mentions a number of the petty states lying round the Eastern end of the Euxine, which had received kings from Trajan or Hadrian, and among them the Lazai, who are probably the same as the Ladii referred to by Capitolinus[3] as receiving a king named Pacorus from Antoninus Pius.

There was thus plenty to engage the attention of the Emperor in the affairs of the East—oppressions by the more powerful states and disputes between rival kinglets, which Antoninus Pius took upon himself to decide, sometimes on his own initiative, sometimes on the invitation of the contending parties, who preferred the justice of his judgments to the arbitration of war[4]. Accordingly Antoninus Pius, who never spared himself in his efforts for the welfare of his empire, visited the East for the purpose of impressing the restless Asiatics with the majesty of the Roman Empire. It has already been shown in the account of the Egyptian rebellion that Capitolinus is wrong, in all probability, when he states that Antoninus never quitted Italy during the tenure of the Imperial power. It will be seen that Antoninus's visit[5]

---

[1] Inscr. Graec. Sic. et Ital. 2314.
[2] Arrian, *Periplus*, 11, 2.   [3] *V. P.* 9, 6.
[4] *V. P.* 9, 7; Eutropius viii. 8.
[5] A belief in another visit of the Emperor to the East is not well-founded. Irenaeus (apud Euseb. *H. E.* v. 20), rebuking Florinus for heresies &c., writes that this was not what they learnt together in their youth at Polycarp's lectures. "For $\pi\alpha\hat{\iota}\varsigma$ $\check{\epsilon}\tau\iota$ $\mathring{\omega}\nu$ in Lower Asia with Polycarp I saw thee, while thou wast faring prosperously $\grave{\epsilon}\nu$ $\tau\hat{\eta}$ $\beta\alpha\sigma\iota\lambda\iota\kappa\hat{\eta}$ $\alpha\mathring{\upsilon}\lambda\hat{\eta}$." $\pi\alpha\hat{\iota}\varsigma$ $\check{\epsilon}\tau\iota$ $\mathring{\omega}\nu$ might be any year up to 30 or 35, while

to the East is tolerably certain, and that the year 155 A.D. may be taken as the approximate date of this visit.

The rebellion in Egypt has been put for various reasons in the year 153 A.D., and Antoninus spent some time in building operations at Alexandria, after the war concluded. It is not probable, then, that he could have left Alexandria[1] on his voyage to Antioch before the beginning of 154 A.D. Now Aristides[2] mentions a dream of his own, which Waddington—basing his calculations on Aristides's testimony as to the state of the malady from which he was suffering—places in the year 155 A.D.[3], the year of the proconsulship of Quadratus in Asia. In this dream, which on the face of it is obviously intended to be a narrative of facts which had recently occurred, Aristides says that he saw Antoninus ὁ πρεσβύτερος coming with a younger Emperor to conclude a treaty with Vologeses, the king of Parthia. This title—ὁ πρεσβύτερος—is the one which Clement of Alexandria[4] uses in order to distinguish Antoninus Pius from M. Aurelius, while

---

to suit the chronology of Irenaeus's life the occasion must have been between 135 A.D. and 150 A.D. The reference to a βασιλικὴ αὐλή in Asia between these years is probably a reference to the proconsulship of Antoninus about 136 A.D. His court was loosely called "royal" by an anticipation of two years—a circumstance easily accounted for, when we remember that Antoninus was marked out by omens during his proconsulship as the future Emperor; cf. *V. P.* 3, 3. Cf. Lightfoot, *Apostolic Fathers*, 2, 1, pp. 429—432.

[1] Malala, xi. p. 280. [2] Arist. (Dind.) 1, 453, 454.

[3] Waddington, *sur la vie d'Aristide* (*Mém. de l'Acad.* 1867, pp. 232—234).

[4] *Stromates*, vii. 17, p. 325.

Tertullian calls Antoninus[1], Antoninus maior. It is therefore probable that Antoninus Pius visited Syria in the latter half of 154 A.D. or the beginning of 155 A.D., taking with him M. Aurelius, and that Aristides has made a mistake in calling Marcus "Emperor" when as yet his title was only "Caesar." This is a very natural mistake, if we remember that there was nominally little difference in position between M. Aurelius, the holder of Tribunicia Potestas, Proconsulare Imperium and the Ius Quintae Relationis, and Antoninus Pius, the actual Emperor. As to the practical difference between the two men owing to the greater age and experience of Antoninus Pius, Aristides clearly points to this by showing that it was the elder of the two who conducted all the negotiations. At any rate there is the express testimony of Malala[2]—not a very credible authority it is true—that Antoninus Pius did at some time visit Syria. Consequently it is better to accept the view that Aristides refers to a visit of Antoninus Pius and M. Aurelius Caesar than to suppose that he is alluding to a visit of the two Emperors, M. Aurelius and L. Verus.

There is very little information with regard to the incidents of Antoninus Pius's visit to Syria. There is in the first place this hypothetical treaty with Vologeses, of which nothing is known beyond the statement of Aristides. Further than this Malala[3] states that Antoninus built baths at Caesarea, paved the streets at Antioch, built a forum and public baths at Laodicea, and erected a temple to Juppiter at Heliopolis in Phoenice Libanus,

---

[1] *ad Marcionem*, 1, 19. [2] Malala, xi. 280.
[3] Malala, xi. 280 and 281.

which was reckoned as one of the wonders of the world. Having thus impressed his foes with a sense of the far-reaching power of Rome and his friends with a sense of the advantages of loyalty, Antoninus Pius returned to Rome before the end of 157 A.D.[1]

There were at this time other matters besides the quieting of the Eastern frontier, which demanded the careful attention of the Roman Emperor. On the North-eastern frontier the Dacians had never really been brought completely into subjection, and at various times during Antoninus Pius's reign either the Dacians themselves or kindred tribes occasioned disturbances, the chief of which seems to have fallen within the years 157—159 A.D.

Practically the only assistance which can be obtained towards fixing the date of the rising, is to be derived from inscriptions, and the information to be obtained from them is necessarily of a somewhat fragmentary nature. At Muntselu Gredistje an inscription[2] of the year 157 A.D. is found running as follows:—"Victoriae Aug. pro salute Imp. Antonini Aug. M. Statius Priscus legatus eius pr. pr." Again an inscription[3] of 158 A.D., found at Brucla, commemorates a vow paid by the same Priscus to Diana: "Dianae Aug. pro salute Imp. Caes. Titi Ael. Hadr. Antonini Aug. Pii P. P. M. Statius Priscus leg. Aug. pr. pr. v.s.l.m." (votum solvit libens merito)—though this may and probably does refer to the payment of the ten-yearly vows, which would fall due in this year. At Apulum another inscription[4]

---

[1] Le Bas et Waddington, *Inscrip. de l'Asie Min.* 866.
[2] *C. I. L.* 3, 1416 (Dacia).   [3] *C. I. L.* 3, 940.
[4] *C. I. L.* 3, 1061.

commemorates the erection in 159 A.D. by a provincial of an altar to Juppiter and the assembly of the gods for the safety of the Roman Empire and the valour of Legio XIII Gemina under M. Statius Priscus, who showed "that the waters must be opened." Similar inscriptions[1] belonging to the same period are found at Napoca, Apulum, and Ad Mediam. It is true that some of these inscriptions may be commemorative merely of the payment of ten-yearly vows[2], which fell due in 158 A.D., but were not publicly paid till 159 A.D.[3]. But it seems impossible to refer others, such as *C. I. L.* 3, 1061 and 1416, in which vows are paid on the one hand for the valour of Leg. XIII, on the other to the Goddess of Victory, to anything but some success gained by the Roman arms. The fact that the payment of the ten-yearly vows for the second period of ten years was postponed till 159 A.D. seems to show that Antoninus's attention was too much engaged in coping with some pressing difficulty for him to have the leisure for paying vows. He wished to feel sure that he was safely through these ten years before he paid the price of the journey through them. Further confirmation for the view that there was serious trouble in Dacia in or soon after the year 157 A.D. is found in the fact that Dacia was divided into three districts instead of two about 158 A.D.[4] in order to render the control exercised by the Roman Emperor more thorough; while for 157 and 158 A.D. M. Statius Priscus[5] was chosen as governor, a

---

[1] *C. I. L.* 3, 860, 1170, 1576.
[2] This is the case with *C. I. L.* 3, 940.
[3] Cf. Eckhel, 7, ad ann. 159 A.D., v. infra.
[4] *C. I. L.* 3, p. xliv.
[5] *C. I. L.* 3, 1061, 1416; and Henzen, 5430.

man whose experience and skill in military matters would mark him out as one eminently fitted for the government of a rebellious province.

The nearest date which can be assigned for the Dacian outbreak is the period between 157 and 159 A.D. Lacour-Gayet[1] puts the rising between 138 and 145 A.D., saying that this is what Aristides refers to in the words "παράνοια Γετῶν," which occur in his 'Ρώμης ἐγκώμιον[2]. Now it is true that the 'Ρώμης ἐγκώμιον is to be placed in the year 145 A.D., and that "Getae" and "Daci" are often used indiscriminately. Yet it is probable that Dacia at this period was continually in a state of disorder, and Aristides may well be referring to some minor outbreak. The probability that Dacia was seldom quiet gains support from what is known of the reorganization of Dacia[3].

We know that by the year 168 A.D. the old division of Dacia Superior and Inferior had been given up in favour of a new division into three districts, called respectively Apulensis, Malvensis and Porolissensis[4]. It is probable that this redivision took place in the year 158 A.D.; for in that year an inscription[5] was set up, containing an address to the soldiers in Dacia, in which after the word "Dacia" followed another word, of which only the syllable "-en-" can now be made out. The missing word is apparently some designation of a district of Dacia, and obviously neither "Inferior" nor "Superior" will do. But the vacant space on each side of the syllable "-en-" is just sufficient to admit of the

[1] Lacour-Gayet, *Ant. P.* 128. [2] Arist. (Dind.) 1, 351.
[3] Cf. for account of reorganization, Lacour-Gayet, *Ant. P.* 129.
[4] *C. I. L.* 3, 1457.   [5] *C. I. L.* 3, p. xliv.

word being supplied as "Malv]en[sis" or "Apul]en[sis." It is therefore probable that the reorganization into three districts was carried out in 158 A.D. under M. Statius Priscus, who was governor in 157 and 158 A.D., —the redistribution being necessary in view of the disturbances which had gone on under the old *régime*.

As to the actual nature and course of the Dacian war nothing is known beyond the remark of Capitolinus[1] that the Dacians revolted and were crushed by the legate of the Emperor. This "legatus Aug. pr. pr." was, as we have seen, M. Statius Priscus[2], who received the consulship in 159 A.D. as a reward for his exertions. Henzen quotes an inscription[3] containing a list of honours enjoyed by Priscus, which it may be advantageous to give in this place:—

M. Stati]o M. f. Cl[audia] Prisco [L]icinio Italico legato Augustorum pr. pr. prov. Cappadociae, leg. Aug[g] pr. pr. prov. Britanniae, leg. Aug[g] pr. pr. prov. Moesiae Super. curato[ri] alvei Tiberis et cloacarum urbis c[os.] leg. Aug. prov. Daciae leg. leg. XIII g[eminae] p[iae] f[idelis] leg. leg. [X]III gem[inae] Martiae Victricis, sacerdoti Titiali [Fl]aviali pr. inter cives et peregrinos tr. pl. quaest. proc. Aug. XX hereditatum prov. Narbonens. et Aquita[niae] [p]r. eq. alae I pr. CR. trib. mil. leg. I adiutr. p. f. et leg. X g. p. [f. e]t leg. IIII Gallicae, praef. coh. IIII Lingonum, vexillo mil. [d]onato a divo Hadriano in expeditione Iudaic[a] Q. Cassius Domitius Palumbus.

It is clear that Antoninus Pius chose one of his most distinguished generals for the governorship of Dacia in 157 A.D., and the choice seems to have been a fortunate one, if we may infer the success of Priscus from his promotion to the consulship in 159 A.D. and to

---

[1] *V. P.* 5, 4.   [2] *C. I. L.* 3, 1061.
[3] Henzen, 5430.

various provincial governorships under the Emperors M. Aurelius and L. Verus.

Nothing more is known of any disturbance occurring in Dacia during the reign of Antoninus Pius, but there were three other outbreaks in the neighbourhood, which point to the insecure state of the North-eastern frontier of the Roman Empire. Gallicanus in his *Life of Avidius Cassius*[1] mentions how Cassius once punished some of his centurions, who had attacked and routed 3,000 Sarmates on the banks of the Danube without having waited for his orders, and how the Sarmates, impressed alike by their defeat and by the severity of Roman discipline, begged for 100 years peace from the "absent Antoninus." There is nothing to show whether this refers to Antoninus Pius or M. Aurelius Antoninus, but it would probably be the former, since Cassius[2] seems to have been in the East during M. Aurelius's reign. If that be so, it is reasonable to connect the defeat of the Sarmates with the subjection of Dacia. The rebellious Dacians had invited assistance from their neighbours the Sarmates, and the latter shared in the discomfiture which befell the former.

Again in the eastern extremity of Dacia the semi-barbarous tribe of the Tauroscythae began a policy of aggression, and attacked the citizens of the neighbouring town of Olbia[3]. The people of Olbia were unable to protect themselves, and a Roman force was sent to their assistance, which drove back the Tauroscythae and compelled this restless tribe to give hostages to Olbia as pledges of peace for the future.

[1] *V. Avid. Cass.* 4, 6.   [2] Cf. *V. Avid. Cassius.*
[3] *V. P.* 9, 9.

Not far from Olbia in the east of Dacia, at some distance north of the mouth of the Danube, there lived at this time a tribe called the Costobocae, who were practically independent of Rome. Pausanias[1] states that during the reign of Antoninus Pius these Costobocae advanced into Greece as far as Elatea in Phocis;—a statement which is nowhere directly corroborated, and which must be regarded with suspicion, since it is almost incredible that a northern tribe could have invaded such a central province of the Roman Empire as Achaia, without having first mastered the districts of Moesia, Thracia and Macedonia. Yet it is possible that the Costobocae may have organized unexpectedly a raid, and have penetrated to Achaia before the Romans grasped the situation; and it may be that Capitolinus[2] refers to some such invasion when he mentions a disturbance in Achaia. Such an invasion, if it did take place, was a sign of great restlessness among the half-conquered nations living to the north of the Danube, and an ominous forerunner of the subsequent descent of semi-barbarous tribes from the North upon the more civilized but weaker inhabitants of the shores of the Mediterranean. Of the invasion neither date nor detail is known, beyond the fact that the Roman forces were able to cope with the emergency[2].

Thus much is known with regard to the troubles on the North-eastern frontier during the reign of Antoninus Pius; and from the facts before us it is reasonable to conclude that during the greater part of this reign the Dacians and the kindred tribes were persistent in their endeavours to disturb the peace of the Roman Empire,

[1] Paus. 10, 34, 2. [2] *V. P.* 5, 5.

until at last, in 158 A.D., Antoninus struck at the root of the matter, and by effecting a reorganization of Dacia ensured to himself peace for the remaining years of his life. There is at least no evidence of any disorder in the provinces between the years 159 A.D. and 161 A.D., while the scanty information which we possess with regard to the general course of events during these years goes to show that affairs at home were equally unimportant and uneventful.

The Emperor's seventh Congiarium had been distributed in 154 A.D., during his absence from Rome; his eighth was bestowed in 158 A.D.[1], after he had returned from the East. In the course of the same year the second period of ten years elapsed, during which Antoninus Pius had been Emperor, and the completion of the 20th year was celebrated like the completion of the 10th by the payment of vows throughout the Empire[2]. However, no official celebration seems to have taken place until the following year 159 A.D., when coins[3] were struck referring to the payment of vows for the second ten years, and the taking of new vows—never to be paid—for the third period:—

{ Antoninus Aug. Pius P. P. Tr. P. XXII. (Head.)
{ Vota Sol. Dec. II. Cos. IIII. s. c. (Emperor with Toga sacrifices at a tripod.)
{ Antoninus Aug. Pius P. P. Tr. P. XXII. (Head.)
{ Vota Suscepta Dec. III. Cos. IIII. (As above.)

Why the old vows were not paid and new vows taken in 158 A.D. is not certain, but it may well be that the

[1] Eckhel, 7, ad ann. 158 A.D.; Cohen, 198.
[2] Cf. *C. I. L.* viii. 765; *C. I. L.* iii. 940, 5166.
[3] Eckhel, 7, ad ann. 159 A.D.

pressure of war and reorganization in Dacia rendered their postponement inevitable.

In the same year another class of coin[1] was struck:—

> Antoninus Aug. Pius P. P. Tr. P. xxii. (Head.)
> Aed. divi Aug. rest. Cos. iiii. (Temple with 8 columns, 2 figures inside, 2 in portico, 2 on steps.)

The temple of Divus Augustus was that which was set up in honour of Augustus when he was canonized, and in which those of the succeeding Emperors, that were canonized, were worshipped[2]—each receiving a chapel or aisle of the main temple. We have seen that Antoninus Pius was engaged in building a temple to Hadrian in 145 A.D. and 151 A.D. It is probable that on the canonization of Hadrian a new temple had to be built to receive the new deity, as the previously canonized Emperors had occupied all the available space in Augustus's temple. In consequence the restoration of the temple of Divus Augustus, mentioned on the coins of 159 A.D., must have been merely the restoration of the ravages of time and not the addition of a new chapel for Hadrian.

Of the remaining months of Antoninus Pius's reign virtually nothing is known. His military activity in all parts of the Empire had secured to him peace for the closing scenes of his life, while his age rendered him unwilling to engage in anything more than the ordinary routine of business at home. This he continued to perform till the end[3], though he gradually relied more

---

[1] Eckhel, 7, ad ann. 159 A.D.   [2] Willems, *D. P. R.* 412 n. 8.
[3] *V. P.* 13, 2.

THE REIGN OF ANTONINUS PIUS.

and more upon the judgement of M. Aurelius[1], who treated his adoptive father with all possible attention and was seldom absent from his side[2]. The end came in the early part of the year 161 A.D., for which year coins of Antoninus Pius were struck bearing the date Tr. Pot. XXIIII.[3] and containing a reference to another Congiarium of Antoninus—the ninth and last of his reign. It has already been shown that Antoninus did not resume his Tribunicia Potestas before Feb. 25th in each year, and accordingly the inscription of Tr. Pot. XXIIII. on his coins proves that he did not die before Feb. 25th, 161 A.D. On the other hand, by March 23rd of this year (X. Kal. Apr.), an inscription[4] was set up dated by the consulship of the *Emperors* M. Aurelius and L. Verus, i.e. by March 23rd Antoninus Pius was dead. Nearer than this it is hardly safe to venture, since the authority of Xiphilinus in his epitome of Dio Cassius's works and that of Clement of Alexandria[5], cannot be regarded as wholly satisfactory, when an exact date has to be fixed. Xiphilinus[6] says that M. Aurelius died XVI. Kal. Apr., i.e. March 17th, 180 A.D.; Clement[7] states that M. Aurelius reigned 19 years and 11 days. Taking these two statements together and reckoning inclusively, we get March 7th, 161 A.D. as the date for the commencement of M. Aurelius's reign and the death of Antoninus Pius—a date which may be correct, but can scarcely be considered as certain.

---

[1] *V. Marc.* 6, 7—8.   [2] *V. Marc.* 7, 2.
[3] Eckhel, 7, ad ann. 161 A.D.   [4] *C. I. L.* x. 1814.
[5] Lacour-Gayet, 437, n. 1, uses these authorities to fix the death of Ant. Pius exactly.
[6] Xiph. *D. C.* 71, 53.   [7] Clement, *Stromates*, 1, 147.

At any rate it is certain that Antoninus Pius died in the year 161 A.D. between Feb. 25th and March 23rd; he died at Lorium[1], which had been his home and the scene of his hours of leisure throughout his reign, and whither he retired when he felt his end approaching. But the actual stroke of death came suddenly[2]. He ate some Alpine cheese at supper and the next day found himself feverish. On the third day, seeing that he was seriously ill, in the presence of his prefects he entrusted the State and his daughter to the care of M. Aurelius, and ordered that the golden statue of Fortune, which always stood in the bedchamber of the reigning Emperor, should be carried into Marcus's chamber. To the tribune, who asked for the daily watchword, he gave the word "Aequanimitas"—a fitting watchword, with which the calm and careful Emperor might pass the gates of Death. Though his mind wandered, yet in his wanderings he still talked of the affairs of State in which his life's interest lay, and spoke of the frontier-kings who had aroused his wrath. To his only surviving daughter Faustina he left his private possessions, though he remembered all his friends and relations in his will. Then at Lorium[3], 12 miles from Rome, he breathed his last, dying[4] as calmly as though he were falling asleep. He died in the 75th year of his age, old in years, yet his loss was felt as though he had been a young man[5].

The Senate had of course no hesitation in deifying an Emperor[6] whose life and character had won the

---

[1] Eutrop. 8, 8.   [2] *V. P.* 12, 4—8.   [3] Orosius, 7, 14, 1.
[4] Zonaras, xii. *P.* 1, 593, D.   [5] *V. P.* 12, 4.
[6] *V. P.* 13, 3 and 4; *C. I. L.* vi. 1012.

admiration of all. All classes of the State vied in honouring his memory, and all the honours won by the best Emperors were bestowed upon him—games, a flamen, a temple and Sodales Antoniniani[1]. He was remembered as one who, as far as in him lay, had refused to shed the blood of citizen or of enemy[2]; as one whose life and reign might well be compared to that of Numa, not only in its devout spirit and its care of religious details, but also in the prosperity and the safety which were its more substantial characteristics.

[1] *C. I. L.* x. 3724. [2] *V. P.* 13, 4.

CHAPTER V.

The Emperor and the Empire.

Hitherto an attempt has been made to trace in historical outline, so far as the information will permit, the sequence of events which led up to the accession of Antoninus Pius and their course during the 23 years of his reign. It is now proposed to examine the personality of Antoninus and to draw a few conclusions as to the nature of his rule and the position in which he stood with regard to the other component parts of the Roman state.

Section 1. Personal Details and Character.

Antoninus Pius[1] was a man of tall stature yet not ungainly, and he seems to have been very careful to preserve a dignity of demeanour, which should suit his high position as Emperor. When he felt the weight of years upon him he took to wearing boards of lindenwood under his clothes in order that he might not stoop. His voice was loud and ringing, but avoided harshness by its pleasant and cheerful tone. His expression was calm and dignified as became his actions and his character[2].

---

[1] *V. P.* 13, 1 and 2.   [2] *V. P.* 2, 1.

Antoninus's tastes were for the most part those of a Roman country gentleman[1], who took great pleasure in fishing and hunting and in conversing with his friends as he walked up and down, and who shared in the rural holidays, such as the vintage-festival, in common with the country people on his estate. He found time to look after the cultivation of his land[2], even when Emperor, and throughout his reign he took care that his table should be supplied by the slaves of his own estates[3], by his own fowlers, his own fishers, and his own hunters. But at the same time Antoninus was not devoid of a liking for the amusements of the town, and in the words of Fronto, "palaestram ingressus est et hamum (v.l. theatrum) instruxit et scurras risit[4]." Capitolinus mentions his love of the theatre[5], and in another passage describes the shows of wild beasts[6] which Antoninus exhibited, while coins[7] of the year 149 A.D. also refer to his love of the amphitheatre.

On the more serious side of his nature Antoninus Pius was very precise, and insisted on investigating all the details of every matter that came before him, so much so that he earned for himself the name of κυμινο-πρίστης[8]. In religious matters he was most devout[9], and never failed to perform the customary sacrifices, except when illness prevented him. An inscription found in Rome refers to his care for all religious ceremonies[10] and to his devout spirit, while the various

---

[1] *V. P.* 11, 2.   [2] *V. P.* 2, 1, "diligens agri cultor."
[3] *V. P.* 7, 5.   [4] M. Corn. Fronto, *de Feriis Alsiniensibus*, p. 226.
[5] *V. P.* 11, 2.   [6] *V. P.* 10, 9.   [7] Eckhel, 7, ad ann. 149 A.D.
[8] Xiph. 70, 3, 3. Zon. xii. P. 1, 593, B.   [9] *V. P.* 11, 5.
[10] *C. I. L.* vi. 1001.

coins which were struck during his reign, descriptive of scenes from the old Roman mythology[1], show that he was attempting to set up a reaction in favour of the old and truly Roman religion as against the newly-imported deities of the East.

Antoninus did not presume on his position as Emperor, and various stories are told illustrating his "civilitas." For example, when he had summoned Apollonius from Calchis to Rome to undertake the education of M. Aurelius[2], Apollonius on his arrival in Rome insisted that Marcus should come to him instead of himself going to Marcus; and Antoninus Pius merely laughed, saying that apparently it was easier to come from Calchis to Rome than to cross the street.

Then again, when Antoninus was in the house of Homullus[3], he admired the porphyry columns and asked where Homullus got them. Homullus replied, "When you enter another man's house, you should be deaf and dumb"; and Antoninus bore this and many similar remarks from Homullus without complaint.

When he or his son was a candidate for office, Antoninus went about as a private individual[4], allowing the Senate—at least nominally—the right of free election. With his friends he consorted freely[5], divesting himself, when in their company, as far as possible of his official position and preserving throughout his reign the simplicity and freedom from self-assertion[6] which might be looked for in a private individual, but were seldom to be found in an Emperor.

---

[1] Eckhel, 7, *Mythological &c. coins of Ant. Pius.*
[2] *V. P.* 10, 4.   [3] *V. P.* 11, 8.   [4] *V. P.* 11, 6.
[5] *V. P.* 11, 4—7.   [6] *V. P.* 7, 6.

Capitolinus in two passages gives a fairly good summary of his character and personality:—"Fuit[1] vir forma conspicuus, clarus moribus, clemens, nobilis, vultu placidus, ingenio singulari, eloquentiae nitidae, litteraturae praecipuae, sobrius, diligens agri cultor, mitis, largus, alieni abstinens, et omnia haec cum mensura et sine iactantia, in cunctis postremo laudabilis et qui merito Numae Pompilio ex bonorum sententia conparatur"; and again: "imperatorium[2] fastigium ad summam civilitatem deduxit, unde plus crevit." Yet it is from the *Meditations* of M. Aurelius that we get the clearest insight into his character, and we may conclude this description with the statement of Marcus as to the influence that Antoninus Pius exercised over him[3]:— "From my father I learnt to keep a quiet spirit and to remain unshaken in my opinions, after first considering carefully; to eschew vain glory and to like work; to give each one his due and to know well the time for action and the time for rest; to avoid immorality, to have common sense, not to be exacting in friendship, to preserve an equal demeanour to my friends in their adversity or prosperity; to make careful investigations both in political and in other matters, and not to be satisfied with a general idea; not to tire of or be too strongly attached to my friends, but to be αὐτάρκης in everything, to be prudent and to avoid all tragic display and flattery; to conduct myself carefully and diligently when in office and to put up with affronts; not to be superstitious nor to court the favour of the mob, but to be sober and sure and no innovator; to like good things

[1] *V. P.* 2, 1—2.   [2] *V. P.* 6, 4.
M. Aur. εἰς ἑαυτ. 1, 16.

but to be able to do without them; to be free from sophistry, boorishness and pedantry, and to be a seasoned, perfect man, uninfluenced by flattery and capable of protecting both myself and others; to honour true philosophers and to tolerate without giving way to all opinions; to be friendly in disposition, not self-assertive; to take proper pride in bodily perfection without foppishness, and so to obviate the need for medicine; to respect all ability; to follow my father's example without seeming to be tied to it; to be staid; to resist bodily infirmities; to be sensible and to adopt the golden mean both in work and play; not to be confused, but to be orderly, vigorous and consistent; and to be able to keep from or enjoy those things which many cannot keep from nor enjoy."

So much for the personal character of Antoninus Pius. As for his character as a ruler, it is better to let the events of his reign speak for themselves. We need only remark that it would be the greatest mistake possible to suppose that Antoninus Pius was a weak and feeble ruler, whose age rendered him incapable of carrying on a vigorous policy. He was not, it is true, a military personage like Trajan, but we have seen that he turned the Roman arms to every province where a display of military force was required. Nor was he behindhand in other matters, and it seems to have been his greatest care that all the business of the State should be conducted as expeditiously as possible. He generally resided in Rome in order that no time might be lost in receiving and answering despatches from all parts of the Empire[1].

[1] *V. P.* 7, 12.

Section 2. *M. Aurelius and L. Verus.*

At the commencement of Antoninus Pius's reign the positions of M. Aurelius and L. Verus were at least nominally equal. Antoninus Pius had adopted both of them by the command of Hadrian[1], and the only difference between them was that of age, Marcus being 17 years old, Lucius 7[2]. However, their actual positions soon became differentiated, a state of affairs which is reflected in the doubt felt by the *Scriptores Historiae Augustae* as to whether L. Verus was adopted by Antoninus Pius or by Marcus Aurelius. L. Verus was, as we have clearly seen, adopted by Antoninus Pius. Yet the fact of a doubt existing shows that while Marcus and Lucius were nominally equal, their actual difference in position rendered this equality very questionable. The difference in position during the early part of Antoninus Pius's reign may be easily accounted for by the difference in age, since Marcus was ready to enter on an official career at a time when L. Verus was still a mere child. But, even when grown up, Verus was never placed on an equal footing with Marcus, and an explanation must be sought in the fact that there was little affection betwen Antoninus Pius and L. Verus[3].

Marcus Aurelius[4] was the nephew of Faustina, Antoninus Pius's wife, and after his adoption by Pius was left in charge of affairs at Rome, when Antoninus Pius went to Baiae to bring back Hadrian's dead body to Rome[5]. Marcus was at this time quaestor, and

---

[1] *V. P.* 4, 5.   [2] *V. M.* 1, 5; *V. Ver.* 2, 10 and 11.
[3] *V. Veri*, 3, 6.   [4] *V. Marc.* 1, 3.   [5] *V. Marc.* 6, 1.

Antoninus soon showed that Hadrian's arrangements for the future of Marcus and Verus were not to be carried out literally. Hadrian had arranged that L. Verus[1] should marry Faustina, Antoninus Pius's daughter, but Antoninus, alleging as an excuse the youth of Verus, set aside this arrangement and betrothed Faustina to Marcus[2], while in 140 A.D. he conferred a further honour on Marcus and selected him at the age of 19, by request of the Senate, to be his colleague in the consulship[3]. At the same time he appointed him "VI VIR turmis equitum Romanorum," made him a member of the priestly colleges and gave him the title of Caesar. Coins[4] of M. Aurelius were struck as early as the year 139 A.D., bearing the titles "Caesar" and "Cos. Des." and in 140 A.D. a new type of coin[5] was struck—

{ Aurelius Caes. Aug(i) Pii F. Cos. (Head.)
{ Pietas Aug. (Instrumenta Pontificia.)

which undoubtedly refers to the admission of Marcus to the priestly colleges. Henceforward coins were struck at various times during Antoninus Pius's reign with the name and titles of M. Aurelius upon them[6].

In 145 A.D. Antoninus Pius again made M. Aurelius his colleague in the consulship[7]; and in the same year Marcus held the position of Master[8] in the college of the Fratres Arvales, and vows were then taken by that body on behalf of the safety of Antoninus and Marcus.

[1] *V. Ver.* 2, 3.   [2] Cf. *V. Marc.* 6, 2.
[3] *V. P.* 6, 9; *V. Marc.* 6, 3; *C. I. L.* vi. 159.
[4] Eckhel, 7, *M. Aur.* ad ann. 139 A.D.
[5] Eckhel, 7, *M. Aur.* ad ann. 140 A.D.
[6] Cf. Eckhel, 7.   [7] *V. Marc.* 6, 4; *C. I. L.* 3, 282.
[8] *C. I. L.* 6, 2085, 2086.

In 146 A.D. Marcus married Faustina, and Antoninus celebrated the occasion by bestowing a donation upon the soldiers[1]. In the following year a daughter was born to Marcus, and in honour of this event he received the Tribunicia Potestas, Imperium Proconsulare extra urbem and the Ius Quintae Relationis[2]. These powers comprised almost the whole authority which lay in the hands of an Emperor and, if we are to follow the usual custom and date the rule of an Emperor from the time of his assumption of the Trib. Pot., we must put the commencement of M. Aurelius's rule in 147 A.D. However, we shall find that Marcus's position was recognized, both by himself and by others, as being subordinate to that of Antoninus, and he cannot therefore be considered as really Emperor until 161 A.D., although it is probable that with the advance of years Antoninus left more and more of the business of government to Marcus.

Marcus's position was in fact the position of an Emperor with this limitation—that he held his power from Antoninus Pius, and consequently any authority he possessed was not his in his own right, but depended on the will of another. It was an impossible position for anyone who was not as trustworthy and as loyal as Marcus was to Antoninus. But since these two understood and trusted each other thoroughly, Antoninus was able to gradually raise the position of Marcus, until by 161 A.D. Marcus was already in full possession of Imperial power, when death removed his adoptive father. The chief nominal difference[3] between Antoninus

---

[1] Mionnet, *Coins of Ionia*, n. 321; *V. P.* 10, 2; *V. Marc.* 6, 6.
[2] Cf. Eckhel, 7, *M. Aur.* ad ann. 147 A.D.; cf. *V. M.* 6, 6.
[3] Cf. Eckhel, 7, *M. Aur.*

and Marcus after 147 A.D. was that Marcus had not the titles "Imperator Caesar...Augustus" and "Pontifex Maximus." But the real position of affairs is clearly shown by a letter to M. Aurelius, in which Fronto[1] says:—"Pater tuus imperii Romani molestias atque difficultates ipse perpetitur, te tutum in tranquillo sinu suo socium dignitatis gloriae omnium rerum participem tutatur." Yet Marcus was already sharing in the honours accorded to Antoninus, for we find an inscription recording vows taken for the safety of Antoninus Pius and M. Aurelius by Chrysanthus[2], manager of the granaries at Puteoli and Ostia, while a similar inscription[3] has been discovered at Napoca in Dacia. Then again the Seviri Augustales of Cures[4] made a presentation to Marcus in 147 A.D., and their example was followed by other bodies and by individuals[5]. In the business of government too, Marcus took a part, and in the restoration of Smyrna after the second earthquake he was the leading spirit[6]. Capitolinus shows clearly the extent of Marcus's influence with Antoninus, when he states that that Emperor almost invariably consulted him before promoting anyone[7]. Yet Marcus was always most deferential in his treatment of Antoninus[8],—so much so that people like Valerius Homullus falsely insinuated ulterior motives[9] for his conduct. But Antoninus knew Marcus too well to have any suspicions[10], and throughout his reign kept Marcus[11],

[1] M. Corn. Fronto, *ad M. Caes.* 3, 6.
[2] C. I. L. x. 1562.   [3] C. I. L. iii. 860.
[4] C. I. L. ix. 4957.   [5] Eph. *Ep.* 5, 1296.
[6] Mionnet, *Coins*, 3, 1296; Philostr. v. *Aristidis*, 582.
[7] V. Marc. 6, 7.   [8] V. Marc. 6, 8.   [9] V. Marc. 6, 9.
[10] V. Marc. 6, 10.   [11] V. Marc. 7, 2.

who was devoted to him, by his side. It was therefore in the natural course of events, when Antoninus Pius on his deathbed entrusted the State to the care of M. Aurelius[1], now consul for the third time[2], and commanded that the golden statue of Fortune, which always stood in the bedchamber of the ruling Emperor, should be carried into Marcus's chamber[3]. By so doing he appointed Marcus as his sole successor, and the Senate confirmed his choice[4]. It was only through the generosity of Marcus that L. Verus was allowed a share in the government after Pius's death.

L. Verus occupied a position totally different from that of M. Aurelius during Antoninus's reign. At the commencement of this reign the marriage arrangements made by Hadrian were upset, and Faustina was given in marriage to M. Aurelius[5], while for the present young L. Verus was left out of consideration. Subsequently—but not before 159 A.D., since Marcus's first daughter was not born till 147 A.D.[6], and 12 years was the earliest age for marriage with Roman girls[7]— Verus was married to Lucilla, daughter of M. Aurelius. For the present he was educated under the eye of M. Aurelius till his 15th year[8]—145 A.D.,—when he assumed the Toga Virilis, an occasion celebrated by a Congiarium to the people[9]. Of the remaining years before 161 A.D. we know very little beyond the fact that he held the quaestorship in 153 A.D.[10], and the

[1] V. P. 12, 5.   [2] C. I. L. vi. 1984.
[3] V. Marc. 7, 3; V. P. 12, 5.   [4] V. Ver. 3, 8.
[5] V. Ver. 2, 3.   [6] V. Marc. 6, 6.
[7] Willems, D. P. R. 59.   [8] V. Ver. 2, 10.
[9] Eckhel, 7, ad ann. 145 A.D.; V. Ver. 3, 1.   [10] V. Ver. 3, 3.

consulship immediately afterwards in 154 A.D.[1], and that he was consul for the second time[2] when Antoninus Pius died. His career seems to have been the inevitable result of his birth, which ensured for him a decent share in official honours. But he had neither the ability nor a warm enough place in Antoninus's affections to secure for himself a more prominent position. Antoninus Pius indeed seems to have ignored Hadrian's wish that L. Verus should ultimately become Emperor[3]; and it was Marcus's free choice that made L. Verus his colleague in the Imperial power.

Section 3. *The Senate.*

Aristides[4] speaks of Rome as being from different points of view an aristocracy, democracy or monarchy; and this may be theoretically true, whatever the actual facts of the case were under the Empire. But during the reign of Antoninus Pius an attempt seems to have been made to make the aristocratic side of the Roman Empire once more an actual reality, and to stem the tide which was setting in the direction of a purely military monarchy. Undoubtedly Antoninus Pius was induced to make this attempt by the influences to which he had been subjected before he became Emperor. We have seen that for 52 years he lived the life of an ordinary well-born Roman, holding the various offices for which he was eligible, and filling the post of a leading senator with credit both to himself and to the Senate. He had little prospect of ever becoming

---

[1] *C. I. G.* 5888. [2] *C. I. L.* vi. 1984. [3] *V. Ver.* 3, 8.
[4] Arist. (Dind.) 1, 360—362.

Emperor until after the death of L. Aelius Verus in 138 A.D., and till this time his sympathies must have been entirely with the Senate. But he knew the weakness of the Senate, and its incapacity for dealing with any business that required careful attention; for he had held under Hadrian the position of IV vir[1], an office instituted by Hadrian for the purpose of taking the management of Italy out of the hands of the Senate. Antoninus Pius would therefore commence his reign with the desire to enhance the dignity of the Senate, and to entrust that body with as much power as it could safely enjoy, but at the same time he knew its weakness and incapacity for any serious work.

Throughout his reign Antoninus Pius did everything that was in his power to increase the dignity of the Senate, both individually and collectively. To individual senators he made presents of money[2], which should enable them to live in a manner suitable to their position; to the Senate as a body he paid due deference on every occasion. He consented to beg from it the canonization of Hadrian with every sign of submission[3], though it was in his power to force the Senate's will. We may indeed allow that the picture presented by the epitomists of Dio Cassius is overdrawn, for they represent the Senate as obstinately refusing the petition, until at last Antoninus in tears threatened to resign his Imperial power, unless his boon were granted. Yet there can be no doubt that Antoninus's attitude emboldened the Senate to express their true sentiments on the matter. Then again Antoninus paid

---

[1] *V. P.* 2, 11.   [2] *V. P.* 8, 4.
[3] *V. P.* 5, 1; Eutrop. 8, 7; Xiph. 70, 1, 2; Zon. xii. *P.* 1, 592 D.

a graceful compliment to the Senate[1], by begging indulgences from it for those whom Hadrian had condemned in his madness,—thereby satisfying the Senate by his clemency, and at the same time making it appear that it was the Senate which was granting an indulgence to others. Again he gave account in the Senate, and by edicts, of all his actions[2],—a concession which might have been of real value, but which at this time, with a Senate accustomed to an autocratic rule, was probably nothing more than a formal privilege increasing the dignity of that body without adding to its power.

As to more substantial concessions, Antoninus reversed the policy of Hadrian and placed Italy once more under the government of the Senate. This fact is nowhere definitely stated, but it may be inferred from the words of Spartianus and Appian[3], who say that Hadrian set up IV *viri consulares* to govern Italy, and from the statement of Capitolinus[4] that M. Aurelius restored them in accordance with Hadrian's policy. It must have been a severe blow to the senators when the administration of Italy was taken out of their hands, and the action of Antoninus Pius in restoring it to them doubtless increased his popularity. But the experiment of Antoninus seems to have been a failure, if we may judge from the fact that Marcus reverted to Hadrian's scheme. Another benefit, which the Senate enjoyed under Antoninus, was that none of its members suffered death by his orders[5]. Augustus had conferred on the Senate the right to try capital charges brought against senators[6];

---

[1] *V. P.* 6, 3.   [2] *V. P.* 12, 3.
[3] *V. Hadr.* 22, 13; Appian, *B. C.* 1, 38.   [4] *V. Marc.* 11, 6.
[5] *V. P.* 8, 10.   [6] Dio Cass. 52, 31; Tac. *Ann.* 13, 44.

but with Emperors such as Nero and Domitian many were put to death after trial before the Emperor, or with no trial at all. Antoninus Pius followed the practice of the better Emperors in putting no senator to death himself, while M. Aurelius[1] allowed the Senate jurisdiction in almost all charges brought against senators. Possibly the greatest boon that the Senate enjoyed at this time was in the diminished power of the freedmen. From the commencement of the 2nd century A.D. the Equites[2] began to supplant the freedmen in the important offices of *a rationibus, a libellis, ab epistulis* &c., and the power of the freedmen was thereby undermined. Antoninus Pius furthered the movement[3], and steadfastly refused to countenance favourites and freedmen. He made himself accessible to all by the removal of these go-betweens, and everything that he did was open and above-board. The result of this was that the senators were spared the humiliation of having to cringe before the court-servants to obtain any privilege they required. The Emperor brought himself into personal contact with the Senate and consulted it on all matters, while that curse of the Roman Empire—the swarm of *delatores*, which flourished when freedmen were in power—was effectually driven away[4], and confiscations were rarer than they had ever been before[5].

The Senate as a whole were ready enough to show their approval of an Emperor who treated them so well. But there were individuals who objected to the govern-

---

[1] *V. Marc.* 10, 1.   [2] Willems, *D. P. R.* 428.
[3] *V. P.* 6, 4 ; Arist. (Dind.) 1, 105.   [4] Arist. (Dind.) 1, 105.
[5] *V. P.* 7, 1.

ment of Antoninus Pius. Of such men Catilius Severus was one. He had been consul twice and was *praefectus urbi*[1], and was an ancestor of M. Aurelius on the mother's side. His high offices had induced him to aspire still higher, and he had thought himself a likely successor to Hadrian[2]. Disappointed ambition caused him to express his dissatisfaction at the adoption of Antoninus by Hadrian, and he paid for his discontent by the loss of his office of *praefectus urbi*. Again, Atilius Titianus attempted to set himself up in place of Antoninus Pius[3], but failed and was put to death by the Senate; and here Antoninus showed his clemency by forbidding the Senate to seek out Titianus's accomplices. Priscianus too was accused of a similar plot[4], but escaped condemnation by suicide, and in his case too Antoninus forbade any further inquiry. Another conspiracy is mentioned by Gallicanus, in which a certain Celsus was the leader, and it seems that here also Pius refused to seek out the accomplices, much to the dissatisfaction of his wife Faustina[5].

But these conspiracies were vain attempts not shared in by the majority of the senators. Indeed they probably sprang from a feeling of discontent with that which would recommend Antoninus to most of the senators, —discontent with the fact that Antoninus Pius was set up in a prominent position, when his past life had been that of an ordinary senator, no more distinguished nominally than the lives of the malcontents themselves. At least the senators as a whole took every opportunity

---

[1] *V. Marc.* 1, 4.   [2] *V. Hadr.* 24, 6 and 7.
[3] *V. P.* 7, 3.   [4] *V. P.* 7, 4.
[5] *V. Avid. Cass.* 10, 1; cf. Aur. Vict. *Epit.* 15.

of heaping honours upon the Emperor. They gave him the name of Pius, and called his wife Augusta[1]; they pressed the title of Pater Patriae[2] upon him, canonized Faustina when she died, and set up statues in honour of her and of Antoninus[3]. With the assent of all they canonized Antoninus Pius on his death and accorded him all the honours which were bestowed upon the best Emperors[4],—a fact in no way to be wondered at when we find that it was remembered of Antoninus Pius that "Senatui tantum detulit imperator, quantum, cum privatus esset, deferri sibi ab alio principe optavit[5]."

Section 4. *The Consilium Principis.*

The Consilium Principis[6] was an organization which dated from the early years of the Roman Empire, when Augustus chose men "cum quibus de negotiis ad frequentem senatum referendis ante tractaret[7]." Dio Cassius[8] states that this body consisted of 15 senators, chosen by lot, the consuls, and one member of each of the other magisterial colleges,—the members holding their position for six months,—and he adds that Augustus καὶ ἐστὶν ὅτε καὶ ἐδίκαζε μετ' αὐτῶν. It is clear then that under Augustus the Consilium was in existence, performing both consultative and judicial duties. Later in his reign, when too old to attend the meetings of the Senate, Augustus was accustomed to summon to his palace a select body[9], consisting of 20

---

[1] *V. P.* 5, 2. [2] *V. P.* 6, 6. [3] *V. P.* 6, 7.
[4] *V. P.* 13, 3 and 4. [5] *V. P.* 6, 5.
[6] cf. Madvig, *der römische Staat*, I. chap. vi. § 7, pp. 570—572.
Suet. *Aug.* 35. [8] Dio Cass. liii. 21. [9] Dio Cass. lvi. 28.

sena ors, holding their position for 12 months, the consuls designate, his adopted grandsons, and Tiberius, with other individuals invited at will for each meeting, and the decisions of this assembly were given the authority of *senatus consulta*. This body apparently superseded the former Consilium; its advantages lay in the fact that, besides the ordinary nucleus of members, special men might be summoned for special business, lawyers for judicial matters, men of affairs for administrative work.

Tiberius seems to have followed in the footsteps of Augustus, "choosing σύμβουλοι[1] to assist in judicial matters, and choosing, in addition to his friends and relations, 20 leading men to assist in the transaction of public business." When Tiberius retired to Capreae this Consilium was dropped, but under Caligula and Claudius the example of Augustus was once more followed[2]. Nero[3] certainly had a council, but he accepted or rejected its advice purely from capricious motives. Titus[4] is said to have chosen "Amici" for his council, and subsequent Emperors consulted with selected senators chosen partly by themselves, partly by the Senate, using them for different matters, but especially in judicial work[5]. Indeed in the case of Trajan there is no record of his ever having consulted them on administrative business[6], though he used them considerably in the trial of many important suits, summoning Pliny on one occasion at least to take part in a trial[7].

---

[1] Dio Cass. lvii. 7; Suet. *Tib.* 55. [2] Dio Cass. lx. 4.
[3] Suet. *Ner.* 15. [4] Suet. *Titus*, 7.
[5] Madvig, *op. cit.* p. 571.
[6] Pliny, *Epp.* (ed. Keil) pp. 167 and 174. [7] Pliny, *Epp.* iv. 22.

Hadrian[1] on his accession found that the Consilium did not rest on a sufficiently stable basis. It is probable that the power of the Senate to nominate some of the councillors had been dropped, for there is no record of such nomination under Trajan or the immediately succeeding Emperors. Probably the Emperor had the sole right of nomination and chose a special body for each occasion, inviting no doubt substantially the same men at all times, but perfectly free to include new individuals, or to leave out those who had attended at former meetings. Hadrian reorganized the Consilium and used it principally for legal business, if we may judge from the following passages:—

"Equites Romanos nec sine se de senatoribus nec secum iudicare permisit. Erat enim tunc mos ut, cum princeps causas cognosceret, et senatores et equites Romanos in consilium vocaret, sententiam ex omnium deliberatione proferret[2]."

"Cum iudicaret in consilio habuit non amicos suos aut comites solum sed iurisconsultos et praecipue Iuventium Celsum, Salvium Iulianum, Neratium Priscum aliosque, quos tamen Senatus omnes probasset[3]."

"Causas Romae atque in provinciis frequenter audivit, adhibitis in consilio suo consulibus atque praetoribus et optimis senatoribus[4]."

"ἔπραττε δὲ καὶ διὰ τοῦ βουλευτηρίου πάντα τὰ μεγάλα καὶ τὰ ἀναγκαιότατα καὶ ἐδίκαζε μετὰ τῶν πρώτων τότε μὲν ἐν τῷ παλατίῳ τότε δὲ ἐν τῇ ἀγορᾷ τῷ δὲ Πανθείῳ καὶ ἀλλόθι πολλαχόθι ἀπὸ βήματος ὥστε δημοσιεύσεσθαι τὰ γιγνόμενα[5]."

Hadrian then seems to have instituted a fairly large

---

[1] Cf. Schurz, *de Mutationibus in Imp. Rom. ord. ab Imp. Hadr. factis*, p. 13 sqq.
[2] Spart. *V. Hadr.* 8.   [3] *V. Hadr.* 18.   [4] *V. Hadr.* 22.
[5] Dio Cass. lxix. 7.

body of men, who were called councillors. They were of two classes:—

    i. Important personages in the State called variously "senatores et equites," "amici aut comites," "consules atque praetores et optimi senatores," and οἱ πρῶτοι.

    ii. Prominent lawyers.

It is worthy of note that Hadrian was the first Emperor to admit equites to the Consilium, but he would not allow them to take part in trials of senators. Similarly it is probable that on each occasion only certain of the councillors were summoned—those, in fact, who were specially qualified to take part in the business of the meeting[1]. The jurisconsults, however, were a permanent part of each assembly[2], for their advice would be necessary as well on administrative as on judicial business. They were retained at large salaries—the more important under the name of "consiliarii Augusti," at a salary of 100,000 H.S., the less important as "adsumpti in consilium," at a salary of 60,000 H.S.[3] Among them would be the *praef. praetorio*, who at this period was always a prominent lawyer[4]. Hadrian asked for the sanction of the Senate to his list of Councillors, but it is unlikely that this sanction was anything more than a purely formal matter. His method of using the Councillors was to ask the advice of all and to discuss questions among them, and then to come to

---

[1] Cf. *V. Alex. Sev.* 16.

[2] It is not necessary to assume that *all* the jurisconsults would be summoned to each meeting; cf. Willems, *D. P. R.* p. 459.

[3] *C. I. L.* vi. 1634, x. 6662; *Dig.* 27, 1, 30.

[4] Momms. ii. 1065, notes 4—6.

a decision himself after considering the advice tendered to him. It seems that the questions submitted were mainly legal, but it is probable that Hadrian used the Consilium for other matters as well. Certainly Antoninus Pius and subsequent Emperors used it for political business[1].

The special point, which has to be considered with regard to Hadrian's use of the Consilium, is that, whereas former Emperors consulted this body for the decision of actual suits, Hadrian used it for the enactment of laws. The continual tendency of the Empire had been to reserve all powers of law-making for the Emperor himself, and this tendency was greatly encouraged by the stereotyping of magisterial edicts in the *Edictum perpetuum* of Salvius Iulianus. Hadrian both increased and improved his own legislative powers by making the Consilium the vehicle of his legislation[2], and henceforward the main legislative changes emanated from the Consilium Principis.

Such was the nature of the Consilium when Antoninus Pius came to the throne. In its chief or legal aspect it was in the first place the highest court of the Empire, and in the second place the source of the chief changes which were made in the law. In its political aspect it had to a great extent superseded the Senate as a deliberative body. The Senate still met, and nominally the decision of questions still rested with it. But when the leaders of the Senate had already discussed all the business in the Consilium, the discussions in the Senate can have had little real meaning.

[1] *V. P.* 6, 11; *V. Marc. Ant.* 22, 3; *V. Alex. Sev.* 16, 3.
[2] *V. Hadr.* 18.

Capitolinus[1] gives a list of the jurisconsults whom Antoninus Pius employed—Vindius Verus, Salvius, Valens, Volusius Maecianus, Ulpius Marcellus and Diavolenus, to whom should be added Gavius Maximus, Tatius Maximus, Fabius Repentinus, and Cornelius Victorianus, since these four men were *praef. praetorio* under Pius[2]. Of these councillors[3], Vindius Verus was *consul suffectus* with another lawyer, C. Pactumius Clemens, in June 138 A.D.[4]; Salvius is probably P. Salvius Iulianus, who under Hadrian arranged the *Edictum perpetuum*, and who was consul with C. Bellicius Torquatus in 148 A.D.[5]; L. Fulvius Aburnius Valens was made *praefectus urbi* at the time of the Feriae Latinae in 118 A.D.[6]—a nominal office often given to young men of high rank at the commencement of their career; L. Volusius Maecianus was appointed legal tutor to M. Aurelius[7]; L. Ulpius Marcellus held the office of *Leg. Aug. pr. pr.*[8] in Pannonia Inferior; while Diavolenus is probably to be identified with Iavolenus Priscus, who came to the front as early as the reign of Domitian and held the proconsulship of Africa in Hadrian's reign[9].

With regard to the use which Antoninus Pius made of his council, Capitolinus[10] states that the Emperor never decided concerning provincial or other matters without first consulting his *amici*, and that he gave all his decisions in accordance with their advice. In another

---

[1] *V. P.* 12, 1.   [2] *V. P.* 8, 7 and 8.
[3] Cf. Roby, *Introd. to Digest*, p. 158 sqq.   [4] *C. I. L.* iii. p. 879.
[5] *C. I. L.* vi. 375, 3885.   [6] *C. I. L.* vi. 1421.   [7] *V. Marc.* 3, 6.
[8] *C. I. L.* iii. 3306, 3307.   [9] *C. I. L.* iii. 2864.   [10] *V. P.* 6, 11.

passage the same writer[1] mentions that numerous legal principles were laid down by Pius, and that these were almost entirely the result of advice from his legal councillors. It is not proposed to give in this essay a detailed account of the various changes effected in the law of Rome by Antoninus Pius. But in a few words it may be said that the modifications introduced by this Emperor were designed for the protection of the weak and for the removal of technical objections which stood in the way of justice. He simplified the laws of inheritance[2] and bequest in order that no formalities might stand in the way of the testator's wishes. In the matter of adoption[3] he provided for the protection of the interests of minors. Unreasonable manumission he checked, but enacted that the grant of freedom, when once legally established, could not be revoked[4], while he made various rules for regulating the relations of master and slave[5]. Many other alterations in Roman law made by Pius might be cited, but those mentioned already will suffice to show the nature of his enactments. They did not contain much that was new, but they were of considerable importance in mitigating the severity, and in removing the sometimes illogical technicalities, which abounded in Roman law[6].

[1] *V. P.* 12, 1.   [2] *Dig.* 40, 5, 42; 29, 1, 9; 29, 1, 15, 2.
[3] *Dig.* 1, 7, 21 and 1, 7, 32, 1.   [4] *Dig.* 5, 3, 7, 2 and 40, 2, 9, 1.
[5] *Dig.* 1, 6, 1, 2 and 29, 5, 1, 5.
[6] I have not thought it advisable to enter into many details as to the modifications in Roman law made by Pius, as this essay is designed to be entirely historical. References to enactments of Pius will be found in Schiller, *Gesch. röm. Kais.* II. p. 630, and the subject is treated fairly fully in Lacour-Gayet, *Antonin le Pieux*, pp. 403—431.

Section 5. Italy.

The reign of Antoninus Pius was not one which produced any result of the first magnitude for the Italians; indeed it would seem that the change of rulers made almost less difference to the Italians than to any other members of the Roman Empire. Antoninus Pius did, as we have already seen, remove the four consular governors of Italy who had been set up by Hadrian, and who ruled each a quarter of the Italian Peninsula. But this was a change which affected rather the dignity of the Senate, to which Italy was again entrusted, than the well-being of the Italians. It is not probable that the Italians noticed any actual change beyond possibly a slight decrease in the punctuality with which their business was performed, and a trace of carelessness in the management of Italian affairs. But if any such causes for complaint arose, they were due to the incapacity of the Senate and not to the inattention of Antoninus Pius, who lived in his earlier years, and also when Emperor, as much as possible on his country estates at Lorium and in Campania[1], and would therefore understand and sympathise with the feelings and wishes of the Italians.

From the commencement of his reign Antoninus Pius was careful to free the Italians from those burdens which would tax their resources. One of his earliest acts was to return to the Italians the whole of the Aurum Coronarium[2], which they offered him in honour

---

[1] *V. P.* 2, 10; 1. 8; 7, 11.
[2] *V. P.* 4, 10; cf. Eckhel, 7, ad ann. 139.

of his accession; while throughout his reign he was always to the fore in assisting various communities to carry out public works[1] which were necessary either for the maintenance or for the development of their townships. For the development of trade and commerce he was always ready to make every effort, and with this object he built a harbour at Caieta[2] and restored another at Tarracina, and carried out and amplified Hadrian's promise to restore a sea-wall at Puteoli[3], building for the purpose a species of pier resting on 20 pillars. With a view to inland trade he built a new bridge[4] over the river Trerus, on the Via Latina, not far from Fregellae. Then again he encouraged the various trades of the Italian towns to form guilds for self-protection, and inscriptions[5] in his honour were set up (e.g. at Ostia) by the guilds of boatmen, scriveners, &c. Nor did Antoninus Pius neglect the comfort or pleasure of his Italian subjects. He built or assisted in the building of baths at Ostia[6], made an aqueduct at Antium, and in 143 A.D. furnished Scylacium[7] with a water-supply from the neighbouring river. At Capua[8] he restored the amphitheatre in accordance with Hadrian's promise, and apparently assisted the Capuans in other public works. Firmum Picenum[9], too, owed the restoration of its amphitheatre to Pius, while at Puteoli[10] a statue was set up in honour of Pius, "constitutori sacri certaminis iselastici," i.e. founder of sacred games, in

[1] *V. P.* 8, 4. [2] *V. P.* 8, 3. [3] *C. I. L.* x. 1640, 1641.
[4] *C. I. L.* x. 6891. [5] *C. I. L.* xiv. 46, 247, 250.
[6] *V. P.* 8, 3; *C. I. L.* xiv. 98, 376. [7] *C. I. L.* x. 103.
[8] *C. I. L.* x. 3831, 3832, 5963. [9] *C. I. L.* ix. 5353.
[10] *C. I. L.* x. 515.

which the victor is conducted home in triumph. His birthplace, Lanuvium[1], he honoured by building there more than one temple. At Laurentum[2] an inscription has been found, which states that Antoninus Pius not only respected but even increased the privileges of that township, but there is no exact record of what he did there. More is known, however, of what was done by Antoninus at Tergeste. Tergeste, the modern Trieste, was a town[3] of fair size, lying exactly at the meeting-point of the trade-routes from Pannonia, Dacia, N. Italy, and the Baltic district, and situated at the same time favourably for Adriatic commerce. In the immediate neighbourhood lived two tribes[4], the Carni to the North, the Catuli to the South,—which Augustus had incorporated[5] with the community of Tergestans, not indeed as citizens either of Tergeste or of Rome, but only " in reditu pecuniario," i.e. in the assessment-roll on which the local taxation was based. Antoninus Pius changed the position of these tribes so as to give them a share in the municipal honours, and thus to impose on them a share of the expenses which had to be defrayed by municipal officers. Yet he did not make them equal to the Tergestans, who were Roman citizens, but probably conferred Latinitas upon them. This is a small matter in itself, but it serves to illustrate the wise policy of the Roman Emperors of the second century A.D. in extending either full or partial citizenship to the subject communities. It was a boon to the Carni and Catuli, who received thereby an improvement in their status.

---

[1] *V. P.* 8, 3. [2] *C. I. L.* xiv. 2070.
[3] Strabo, 7, 5, 2; Velleius, 2, 110. [4] Pliny, *Epp.* 3, 20, 13.
[5] *C. I. L.* v. 532.

It was an equal boon to the Tergestans, who found in their newly-incorporated fellow-townsmen some who could take a share in bearing the expensive burdens of municipal office.

For the burdens of office were very heavy in the towns of Italy, and none but the rich could afford to hold magistracies there. The chief duties of municipal magistrates seemed to be the exhibiting of games, the giving of banquets, and the undertaking of public works. Thus at Fagifulae[1] Q. Parius Severus was appointed II vir *Quinquennalis,* and in honour of his appointment he had to give a banquet to his fellow-townsmen, and to make a present of 8 sesterces to each Decurio and Augustalis, of 3 sesterces to each Martialis or incorporated worshipper of Mars, and of 2 sesterces to each member of the Plebs. An inscription records a similar case at Auximum[2], and parallels may be found in the inscriptions of nearly every township of Italy.

To lighten such burdens Augustus had instituted in Italy and the provinces the *Ordo Augustalium*[3], and nearly every township of Italy contained men of this class. Being almost entirely freedmen they were excluded from municipal office and exempted from the expense attaching thereto, but in virtue of their *Augustalitas* held a certain social rank and quasi-official position, and were called upon to take their share in the burdens of the township. The local Senate nominated each year six men called *Seviri Augustales*, and

---

[1] *C. I. L.* ix. 2553. [2] *C. I. L.* ix. 5823.
[3] Cf. Willems, *D. P. R.* 502.

these men during the year were called upon to give games and banquets, and to deposit a certain sum of money in the local treasury[1]. During their year of quasi-magistracy they wore the *praetexta*, were escorted by two lictors with *fasces*, sat in the law-courts on the *bisellia*, and had a place of honour at the public games. The past and present Seviri Augustales formed the Ordo Augustalium, which was recognized in the second century A.D. as a corporation possessing a chest of its own, and voting grants for statues etc.[2]. This Ordo Augustalium certainly took some of the expense off the shoulders of the municipal magistrates, and private individuals also spent their money freely. At Gabii[3], Aquaia Priscilla, who was a priestess in the town, restored the temple of Spes, exhibited games and gave garments to the poorer citizens. Nor were the townsmen ungrateful, for they voted a statue in honour of Priscilla. But it is to be noted that she paid for the statue herself, while other examples of people paying for their own statues are found at Volternum and at Suessa[4].

Undoubtedly then, in spite of all that could be done, life in the country became a more expensive matter to prominent Italians than life in Rome itself. The result was certain. Italians of distinction deserted the country for Rome, or refused to take part in the municipal government. If they did stay and take their share in the government of their town, their wealth was wasted in an outlay on baths, theatres or games,—

---

[1] *C. I. L.* ii. 2100.
[2] *C. I. L.* v. 4426.
[3] *C. I. L.* xiv. 2804.
[4] *C. I. L.* x. 3724, 4750.

120 THE REIGN OF ANTONINUS PIUS.

from which a two-fold evil resulted. In the first place, the wealth which might have been employed in the development of trade and agriculture was recklessly dissipated. In the second place, the idlers of the Italian towns were encouraged to drift into the position of the mob of Rome, which cared for nothing beyond "panem et Circenses." The Roman Empire is said to have been improved by Hadrian's decentralizing tendencies, but the only present sign of decentralization was the repetition of Rome's vices in many hitherto industrious towns.

Perhaps one of the most typical features of Antoninus Pius's reign was the growth of the charitable endowments for the maintenance of boys and girls. It was not at all a new thing, for even under Nerva special funds had been established for the purpose[1], while in Trajan's reign C. Plinius Secundus had left money to the township of Comum for the maintenance of 100 freedmen[2]. Trajan himself was the first to systematically couple the charitable endowments with loans to farmers; and as Antoninus Pius probably followed in the footsteps of Trajan, it may be as well to give an outline of Trajan's scheme here. This scheme is set forth in a long inscription[3] found at Veleia, near Placentia, which contains a list of farms in the neighbourhood of Placentia, an account of the money lent on each by Trajan, an account of the payment required on these loans and of the distribution among the children. From the inscription it appears that the value of the

---

[1] Schiller, *Geschichte*, 1, 541. [2] C. I. L. v. 5262.
[3] C. I. L. xi. 1146.

farm had to be stated to the *Quaestor Pecuniae Alimentariae*, appointed for the purpose of managing the scheme; and that not more than one-tenth of the value of the farm was ever advanced in these permanent loans. Interest at 5 p.c. was charged on the loan, and the proceeds were divided between the poor children. The inscription quoted contains two schemes:—

    (i) Ch. 1—46.
        Money advanced = 1,044,000 H.S.
        Interest at 5 p.c. = 52,200 H.S. per ann.

Pueri legitimi	245 at 16 H.S. per mens.	= 47,040 H.S. per ann.
Puellae legitimae	34 „ 12 „	„	=	4896 „	„
Puer spurius	1 „ 12 „	„	=	144 „	„
Puella spuria	1 „ 10 „	„	=	120 „	„

                            Total 52,200 H.S. per ann.

    (ii) Ch. 47—52.
        Money advanced = 72,000 H.S.
        Interest at 5 p.c. = 3600 H.S. per ann.

Pueri legit.	18 at 16 H.S. per mens.	= 3456 H.S. per ann.
Puella „	1 „ 12 „	„	=	144 „	„

                            Total 3600 H.S. per ann.

The recipients had to be in the case of boys between 9 and 18 years of age, in the case of girls between 9 and 14[1]; and it is probable that this was so under Antoninus Pius's scheme. The charitable endowments seem to have been gradually growing in number. Pius added to them by instituting Puellae Faustinianae in honour of his wife Faustina[2], and by his time mention had been made in inscriptions of charitable endowments at Atina, Abellinum, Abella, Vibo, Caieta, Anagnia, Fundi, Cupra Montana, Industria, Brixia, Aquileia,

---

[1] Dio Cass. lxviii. 5.   [2] *V. P.* 8, 1.

Compsa, Aeclanum, Allifae, Aufidena, Cures, Auximum and other places[1]. In most of these cases the Quaestors, who administered the endowments, were officers who had held or who held then or subsequently the highest local magistracies. At Aquileia[2] a " praefectus alimentorum" occurs, who apparently had control over all the charitable endowments within that district.

These charitable endowments were widespread throughout Italy. How far they were good is another question. They undoubtedly pauperized Italians and lightened unwisely the responsibility of parents for the maintenance of their children. But they must certainly have been of assistance to farmers, and have supplied them with the capital necessary for successful agriculture. In so far as they did this, they must be regarded as praiseworthy institutions, whose pauperizing influence was outweighed by the benefits which they conferred on the farmers of Italy.

Section 6. *The Provinces.*

Appian, writing in the reign of Antoninus Pius or at some date not far distant from that time, is loud in his praises of the wisdom of the Roman Emperors, and of the prosperity which resulted to the Empire from their prudent measures. "We have," says Appian[3], "now been under the rule of Emperors for close upon 200 years, and during that time the city of Rome has

---

[1] *C. I. L.* x. 330, 1138, 1208, 1216, 47, 4570, 5920, 5928, 6243; *C. I. L.* ix. 5700; *C. I. L.* v. 7468, 4384, 865; *C. I. L.* ix. 981, 1415, 2354, 2807, 4976, 5849, 3434, 3438, 3384.
[2] *C. I. L.* v. 865.   [3] Appian, *Proem.* 7.

been adorned, the revenues of the Empire have increased, and the continued efforts which have been made for peace have resulted in the establishment of happiness and secure prosperity throughout the world. The Emperors have added some new lands to their possessions, and have subdued revolts. But generally speaking their desire has been to improve the territory which they already possessed, rather than to extend their dominion over poor and worthless countries. I myself have seen the sovereigns of some countries coming and offering to be incorporated in the Roman Empire, but refused by the Emperor as likely to be more trouble than they were worth. Over many peoples the Emperors have appointed kings; for some of their subjects they have spent more than they have received. They surround their Empire with huge camps and guard all the land and sea, which lies inside, as though it were a fort." Such are the words of Appian with regard to the nature of the Roman rule, and it is probable that they were written with special reference to the reign of Antoninus Pius.

It is not necessary to go minutely into the relations existing between Antoninus Pius and the peoples outside the Roman Empire; that subject has been already treated in the accounts of the various wars carried on in this reign. But, to speak generally, he had great influence with foreign nations[1], though he loved peace, and, like Scipio, preferred[2] to save one citizen rather than to kill a thousand enemies. He was equally honoured and feared by friendly kings, and many barbarous nations

---

[1] *V. P.* 9, 10.   [2] *V. P.* 7, 12.

laid down their arms, submitting their disputes to his arbitration and abiding by his award[1].

Within the actual limits of the Roman Empire the reign of Antoninus Pius seems to have been blessed with a prosperity which was never equalled under other Emperors. But it must be remembered that Aristides, from whom most of the information on this point is derived, writes in a most exaggerated style and can seldom be trusted implicitly. Yet everything that is known of this period shows that the reign of Pius was a most fortunate one for the Roman provinces, and therefore it may be concluded that Aristides in this case is nearer the mark than usual. He states[2] that under Pius the whole world was in holiday, the blessings of freedom were enjoyed by all, and jealousies between city and city were unknown. Every provincial town gloried in gymnasia, fountains, schools, colonnades and temples, and the Roman Empire seemed like some vast garden of pleasure. The earth was a common mother to all, and the remotest corner of the Empire was a fatherland to everyone that acknowledged the sway of Rome. The trade of Rome[3] extended to the most distant parts of the earth, and the nations of the West exchanged their merchandise for that of the inhabitants of the far East. Travelling by land or by sea was a matter of no difficulty, since the government of Rome had secured peace and order throughout the Empire[4]. When Aristides condescends to come down to details he tells of the richness of Corinth, and dwells in terms

[1] Aur. Vict. *Epit.* 15; Eutrop. 8, 8; Suidas, s. v. *Antoninus.*
[2] Arist. (Dind.) 1, 363—368.   [3] *Ib.* 1, 325—327.
[4] *Ib.* 1, 111—112.

of extravagant praise upon the prosperity of Alexandria, the jewel of the Empire[1], and of Asia Minor, and especially Ionia[2]. He was fairly well qualified to speak of the province of Asia, for he had travelled there considerably[3], and in the course of his wanderings had come into contact with Claudius Severus[4], a native of Phrygia, who held the proconsulship of Asia in 153—154 A.D. This Severus was a man of lofty and devout character, and was remarkable for the resolute way in which he kept to his decisions once made. It is probable that the prosperity of Asia Minor was due in no small degree to the good government of Severus. Orosius[5] confirms the statements of Aristides as to the general prosperity of the Empire under Antoninus, saying that this Emperor governed the State so peacefully and righteously that he was justly called Pius and Pater Patriae. Pausanias[6] goes a step further, and says that Pius should have been called also the Father of Mankind, while Capitolinus[7] states that all the provinces flourished under his rule.

Of the methods of his government little is known which can be said to distinguish his rule from that of other Emperors. He lived for the most part in Rome[8] in order that he might be in a central position for receiving and answering communications from all parts of the Empire; and he was careful to consult his council before deciding on provincial matters[9]. It was his great object to leave the provinces in as quiet a

---

[1] Arist. (Dind.) 1, 39 and 40. [2] Ib. 1, 363. [3] Ib. 1, 505, 523 and 524.
[4] Waddington, *sur la vie d'Aristide* (*Mém. de l'Acad.* 1867, p. 230).
[5] Oros. 7, 14.   [6] Paus. 8, 43, 5.   [7] V. P. 7. 1.
[8] V. P. 7, 12.   [9] V. P. 6, 11.

state as possible, and with this in view he superseded on his accession none of Hadrian's legates, while during his reign he kept good governors in their provinces for seven or nine years[1].

It was always one of Antoninus Pius's first cares to free the provincials as far as possible from all burdens which oppressed them, and to avoid adding any new burdens to those which they already bore. Immediately on his accession he found an opportunity of showing his friendship to the provinces, and returned to them half of the Aurum Coronarium[2] which they had hastened to offer to their new Emperor. Again, throughout his reign he took every precaution to prevent any oppression of the provinces in the collection of tribute[3]. He ordered his procurators to beware of giving the least cause for complaint, and called them sharply to account if they exceeded their duty. He objected most strongly to enriching himself or the Treasury at the expense of the provinces[4]. He was ever ready to listen to complaints brought by provincials against his procurators[5], and compelled the children of any who were convicted of extortion to refund their fathers' ill-gotten gains to the provincials[6]. To ensure that matters were carried out satisfactorily, he himself took pains to gain all possible information with regard to the provinces and the taxes due from them[7]. In other ways he looked after the interests of the provincials by diminishing the taxes[8], and by lightening the burden of the Imperial Post[9]. Aristides speaks in

[1] V. P. 5, 3.   [2] V. P. 4, 10.   [3] V. P. 6, 1.
[4] Zon. xii. P. 1, 593 B.   [5] V. P. 6, 2.   [6] V. P. 10, 7.
[7] V. P. 7, 8.   [8] Arist. (Dind.) 1, 104.   [9] V. P. 12, 3.

praise of the Post[1], and from the Imperial point of view it may have been a good organization, but with careless Emperors it was much abused, and Romans toured through the provinces by means of it at the expense of the provincials. Antoninus Pius put a stop to this abuse of the Post, nor would he go on any tours himself[2], for he knew that the maintenance of the train of an Emperor, however careful he might be, was a burdensome matter to the provinces through which the journey was made.

Besides showing diligence in the removal of burdens from the shoulders of the provincials, Antoninus Pius aided many cities and districts to undertake new public works[3]. His efforts to restore the damage caused by the earthquakes in Asia Minor, and his energy in making roads in S.E. Gaul, have already been noticed. Other examples of his generosity are mentioned by various writers, and in the inscriptions of almost every province of the Empire. At Epidaurus[4] he built a bath of Asclepius, a temple to the Bountiful Gods, a temple to Hygeia, Asclepius and Apollo, a reservoir for water, and other buildings; while he restored the porch of Cotys, which had suffered from the weather, and put a new roof over the main temple of the Healing God. At Athens he completed an aqueduct[5] which had been commenced by Hadrian; and Corcyra, Delphi, Thespiae and Chaeronea all had cause to be grateful for his bounty[6]. In 157 A.D. at Porolissum in Dacia he restored, by the agency of his procurator Ti. Claudius

---

[1] Arist. (Dind.) 1, 336.   [2] *V. P.* 7, 11.   [3] *V. P.* 8, 4.
[4] Paus. 2, 27, 7.   [5] *C. I. L.* iii. 549; *C. I. G.* 347.
[6] *C. I. G.* 1879 b; *Inscr. Gr. Septentr.* 1050, 1842, 3419.

Quinctilianus, the amphitheatre which had fallen out of repair[1]; and after a fire had caused considerable damage at Narbo, he built a bath and colonnade in that city at his own expense[2]. In Numidia he restored the temple of Neptune at Lambaesis in 158 A.D., and rearranged the water-supply for that town[3], while at Verecundia an aqueduct was built either at the expense of, or at least on the suggestion of Pius[4]; and a triumphal arch erected in his honour at Sufetula in Byzacium shows the esteem in which he was held throughout the district[5].

One of the chief merits of Pius's reign lay in the fact that he was easily accessible to all his subjects[6], and that the intervention of freedmen was not necessary for the obtaining of any request. Individuals and deputations came from the provinces and laid their grievances before Antoninus Pius, and he examined their cases personally. For instance, the district-council of Tarraco either came in a body or sent a deputation to wait upon Pius[7]; and again from the Pagus Lucretius, near Arelate in Gallia Narbonensis, Q. Corn. Zosimus[8], a VI *vir Augustalis*, journeyed to Rome in the interests of his town, and spent several years there. He brought to the notice of Antoninus Pius that the *Pagani* were being excluded from the use of the public baths, and the *sacratissimus princeps omnium saeculorum* restored to them their former privileges.

[1] *C. I. L.* iii. 836.
[2] *V. P.* 9, 2; *C. I. L.* xii. 4342.
[3] *C. I. L.* viii. 2652, 2653.
[4] *C. I. L.* viii. 4205.
[5] *C. I. L.* viii. 228.
[6] Arist. (Dind.) 1, 105.
[7] *C. I. L.* ii. 4055.
[8] *C. I. L.* xii. 594.

Many were the cases in which Antoninus Pius was called upon to adjudicate on disputes arising in the provinces. Some citizens of Thebes were in dispute with the town of Plataea[1] as to the possession of some land which lay between the towns of Plataea and Thebes. Being unable to settle the matter by agreement, they brought the dispute at last before Pius, and he decided the issue. Again, some people of Thisbe[2] had encroached on the land of the Coroneans in Boeotia, and the Coroneans in consequence had taken pledges from the property of the Thisbeans. Antoninus Pius arbitrated that the Thisbeans should pay for the occupation of the land, and that, when payment was made, the pledges should be restored. Other cases could be cited in which Pius was called upon to decide difficult questions. The justice of his decisions was never questioned[3], and according to Aristides he invariably left both parties satisfied with his verdict[4].

There is little more that need be said with regard to the provincial rule of Antoninus Pius. Prosperity seemed to wait on his government, and it was perhaps not entirely due to him that his Empire flourished so remarkably. Yet he was not a little responsible, and strained every nerve to make his provinces contented. Nothing was too trivial for his investigation. Was it a question of framing rules for a festival at Smyrna[5], Antoninus gave the matter his personal attention. Did Carthage require some change in the flow of water[6]

---

[1] *Inscr. Gr. Septentr.* 2415, 2416.
[2] *Ib.* 2870.
[3] Arist. (Dind.) 1, 104.
[4] *Ib.* 1, 337, 369.
[5] *C. I. G.* 3175.
[6] *Eph. Ep.* 7, 696.

which supplied the public baths, it was Antoninus who gave orders for the work. In fact every detail of life in every province of his Empire was a care to this conscientious ruler; and therefore, though he may not have been a man of transcendent ability, yet Antoninus Pius was only reaping his due reward in the general happiness and prosperity of his dominions.

Section 7. *Men of letters.*

It is a phenomenon which may frequently be observed in the history of literature, that, when a nation is struggling for existence or is distracted by the troubles of civil commotion, the struggle or commotion itself seems to call into being those glorious intellects whose utterances have ennobled the age to which they belong. On the other hand, when peace and progress have made smooth the path to literary eminence, the very ease and security of the times seem to stifle the utterance of literary men and to remove all the grit and backbone from their works. A Demosthenes may lead Athens in her final struggles; it is left to Aristides to write declamations in the prosperous reign of Antoninus Pius. For the reign of Antoninus Pius was on the whole peaceful and prosperous, a period specially suitable for the flourishing of art and literature. The Emperor himself was, in the words of Capitolinus[1], "vir......ingenio singulari, eloquentiae nitidae, litteraturae praecipuae," and he was not slow to reward with honours or with money the orators and rhetoricians of every province[2]. The result was what might have

[1] *V. P.* 2, 1.   [2] *V. P.* 11, 3.

been expected,—a literary spirit spread throughout the Empire, and numerous writers of second-rate ability arose. It is hard to find an author of this period—save perhaps Lucian—who has any claims to be regarded as first-rate. It is altogether impossible to discover a single one who may be considered great. Several writers of this age there are whose compositions are interesting and at times even brilliant, but at best they seem only to be echoing the great voices of the past and to be living on the literary capital of the world without adding thereto any new creative idea of their own.

Among these writers, undoubtedly the first place must be assigned to *Lucian*, a native of Samosata in Commagene, who had travelled in Syria, Greece, Italy and Gaul, and in the course of his travels had learnt enough shrewdness to make the best display of the knowledge he possessed. He is a very bright writer of smart essays, and endowed with a keen appreciation of the defects of human nature. Fertile in the invention of strange scenes, humorous and blessed with a good style, he is shrewd rather than deep, and ridicules not principles but persons. He cares little for the truth of what he says, provided only he can sting sufficiently sharply. Yet his satire always has some foundation to go upon, for he is too clever to allow himself to be ridiculous. Lucian in the first place satirizes the *Greek and Roman Mythology*[1], and draws a picture of an auction at which the celestial properties are knocked down for a mere song. Zeus is at one time represented as a petulant old man, who finds the task of ruling the world too hard for him, and wonders why mortals envy him his state; at

---

[1] Ζεὺς τραγῳδός, etc.

another time Zeus's existence is altogether denied. The opinion that the gods are happy came from Homer, and he of course could not even see things on earth. The prayers of men come through the floor of heaven by means of vent-holes, and Zeus, when he feels inclined, removes the covers from these holes just to hear what men are talking about[1], but he will not answer the prayers favourably unless he gets a good bribe. In the second place Lucian ridicules *Philosophers*[2] who—whether Cynics, Stoics or what not—inveigh against wealth and luxury in their time of poverty, but, when their fees have grown, live in a style which would suit a Croesus. They are all rogues, who have not the slightest care for the views which they profess; their only desires are to get large fees for their bad instruction and to attack each other. Lastly Lucian satirizes those *Eastern religions*, whose chief characteristics were extravagant excesses and theatrical displays; and here he is not careful to distinguish between the worship of Mithras and of kindred deities and the religion of *Christianity*. He confuses these two different types of religion in an attack on Christianity[3], as exemplified in Peregrinus Proteus. Proteus is described as a low profligate who had killed his parents and committed other offences, in consequence of which he fled to Palestine. Here he joined the Christians and became a great man among them, holding all their offices καὶ πάντα μόνος αὐτὸς ὤν. He expounded their scriptures and gave them new laws, but was cast into prison by the provincial governor. However, he was visited by

---

[1] Ἰκαρομένιππος.   [2] Βίων πρᾶσις. Ἁλιεύς.
[3] περὶ τῆς Περεγρίνου τελευτῆς.

Christians of both sexes and posed as a new Socrates, till the governor, not wishing to make a hero of him, set him at liberty. Proteus now returned to his home, where he found that he was in ill odour for the murder of his parents. But on making over his property to the Christians he was immediately restored to favour. Eventually he was expelled from the Christian body for eating forbidden meats, and he then wandered about as a Cynic, committing every variety of semi-religious excess. He ended his life by leaping with great parade on a pyre, at the Olympian games, in 165 A.D., and superstitious people said that an eagle rose from his pyre crying "ἔλιπον γᾶν, βαίνω δ' ἐς Ὄλυμπον."

Besides being a satirist of no mean order, Lucian had considerable renown as a writer on more serious subjects; his Χαρών contains many grave reflections, while the Λεξιφανής gives good hints on style. But it is as a satirist that Lucian is principally known. His genius was a destroying power, which stripped everything bare of all pretence, while at the same time it turned the substance to dust. He unintentionally furthered the progress of Christianity not a little, as he demonstrated that Zeus was no god, and that the existing Philosophy was valueless. Room was thus made for the growth of a new religion, and it was not long before Christianity with its militant principles began to occupy the space which Lucian had so opportunely cleared before it.

Apuleius of Madaura, a town on the borders of Numidia and Prov. Africa, was another well-known writer of the period. He was the son of a rich provincial, and inherited 1,000,000 H.S.[1] Educated first at Carthage, he subsequently moved to Athens[2], where he became attached to Platonism. After his education was completed, he travelled[3] through Italy, Greece, and Asia, becoming acquainted with numerous kinds of religions and being initiated into all sorts of mysteries. Finally he set out for Alexandria, but on the way fell ill, was received into the house of a friend, Sicinius Pontianus, and at last arranged to marry Sicinius's mother[4]. But Herennius Rufinus, a relation of Sicinius's family, accused him of winning the lady's affections by spells, and brought him before Claudius Maximus, proconsul of Africa. Apuleius on this occasion delivered his Apology and was acquitted. Afterwards he settled down in Africa, and had at various times the charge of exhibiting wild-beast shows and gladiators, and statues were set up to him by several towns of the province[5]. The dates of his birth and death are uncertain, but we know that he was alive during Antoninus Pius's reign from his references to Lollius Urbicus, Lollianus Avitus, and other distinguished men of the time[6]. His principal works are :—

i. *The Metamorphoses*, or *The Golden Ass*, a romantic account of the transformation of a certain Lucius of Madaura into the form of an ass. In this work Apuleius finds occasion to satirize the manners and life of the priests of various religions and to expose their hypocrisy and fraud. It is probable that his attack is directed especially against Christians, since it was

[1] *Apol.* 443.
[2] *Florid.* iv. 20.
[3] *Apol.* 494.
[4] *Apol.* 534—560.
[5] *Florid.* iii. 16.
[6] *Apol.* 381, 444, 445.

the custom to ridicule Christians as the worshippers of an ass.

ii. The *Apology*, containing some account of his life and of the people with whom he had come into contact.

iii. *Florida*, which has been regarded as a species of commonplace book, but which is more probably a series of extracts from his works by one of his admirers.

As a whole Apuleius is lively, witty, acute and eloquent, many-sided and full of fancy; but he lacks originality and is too discursive to be a great writer. His *Metamorphoses* contain many comic and thrilling scenes, and include stories derived from the legends of the different countries which Apuleius visited; but his work is disfigured by an underlying tone of immorality. His style of writing is fairly good, but it is spoilt by its forced conceits and studied artificiality, while obsolete and unusual words are dragged in at every turn. Apuleius wishes to exhibit his learning, and he therefore loses that simplicity which is characteristic of true art.

The writings of *Aristides* are a lamentable sign of the absence of free thought and free expression among the literary men of the second century A.D. Romans had become accustomed to a despotism, benevolent now, it is true, but none the less a despotism, and consequently all practical interest in public life was gone. Public affairs were managed for the good of the people, but not by the people. Semblances of freedom might be preserved and Antoninus might restore the government of Italy to the Senate, but whether it was nominally the Senate or nominally the Emperor who ruled, the real power was always in the hands of the latter. P. Aelius Aristides therefore, though an orator, does not really touch on practical politics. He celebrates the glories of Athens[1] in a long panegyric, and in like manner showers his praises upon Rome[2]. He discusses the question whether the Athenians ought to have sent the Sicilian expedition, and puts speeches on the subject into the mouths of Athenians and others of that time. He writes speeches from the different points of view of the various combatants at the battle of Leuctra, books on religious cures effected in the temples throughout the Roman Empire, and, to satisfy the prevailing semi-religious spirit, he composes addresses to the gods. All this he does in a purely academic fashion absolutely remote from any possibility of practical result. His style is excellent, in spite of a certain artificiality, and in comparison with many writers of his time his matter may be considered as fairly interesting. But his great defect is his exaggeration. His admirers compared him to Demosthenes, and therein paid the worst of all compliments to the literature of their time; for if Aristides stood in the same relation to contemporary literary men in which Demosthenes stands to all other orators, it needs little insight to infer that the literature of the middle of the second century A.D. must have been of the most feeble and worthless nature.

The eclectic spirit of the times is well exhibited in the writings of *M. Aurelius*. Eclecticism is an almost inevitable characteristic of every age, which succeeds a period of literary and intellectual activity, unless the succeeding age is sufficiently vigorous to turn men's

[1] Arist. (Dind.) 1, 150—321. [2] *Ib.* 1, 321—371.

attention from the past to the present. If it be not strong enough, men are left to cull what they will from the great authors of the past and have not the power to assimilate such extracts into their own being and to send them forth once again fresh and living. Of such eclecticism M. Aurelius is a good example. He tabulates the various lessons which he received from those teachers—mainly Stoics—who influenced his early years, and the result is that when we read his writings he seems to be repeating a lesson which he has learnt by heart, rather than to be uttering the feelings of his mind. Yet there was a natural steadiness and sobriety at the bottom of his character which specially fitted him for the reception of Stoic ideas, and therefore he is at times seen in the light of a true Stoic and not in that of a parrot repeating Stoic sentiments. At least he is always conscientious, earnest and thorough, and this may to some extent compensate for a lack of backbone and personal vigour in his writings. His *Meditations* have no claim to literary merit; indeed they were not written with a literary aim, but were intended to serve as a species of philosophical diary or handbook to supply information and advice on many important questions of daily life. At one time he thanks Rusticus, who turned his mind from the tricks of rhetoric and empty smartness towards τὸ ἀκριβῶς ἀναγιγνώσκειν καὶ μὴ ἀρκεῖσθαι περινοοῦντα ὁλοσχερῶς[1]. At another time he expresses his gratitude to Apollonius, who taught him to look to reason alone and always to keep the same temperament whether in joy or sorrow[2]. He gives a long list of the lessons which he learnt from Antoninus

[1] M. Aur. εἰς ἑαυτ. 1, 7.   [2] *Ib. id.* 1, 8.

Pius[1], of which the chief seem to have been moderation and self-sufficiency. All of his writings have a sober earnestness in them, and the principles set forth seem to be those by which M. Aurelius regulated his own life:—συζῆν θεοῖς, ἔσω βλέπε, μὴ διαφέρου πότερον ῥιγῶν ἢ θαλπόμενος τὸ πρέπον ποιεῖς, ὁ ἀδικῶν ἀσεβεῖ, ὁ ἁμαρτάνων ἑαυτῷ ἁμαρτάνει[2]. Or again, they were principles which would enable a man to play honourably an important part in political life:—

ὅπου ζῆν ἐστιν, ἐκεῖ καὶ εὖ ζῆν· αὐλῇ δὲ ζῆν ἐστιν· ἔστιν ἄρα καὶ εὖ ζῆν ἐν αὐλῇ[3].

ὅρα μὴ ἀποκαισαρωθῇς· μὴ βαφῇς[4].

λαλεῖν καὶ ἐν συγκλήτῳ καὶ πρὸς πάνθ' ὁντινοῦν κοσμίως, μὴ περιτράνως· ὑγιεῖ λόγῳ χρῆσθαι[5].

Enough quotations have been given to show the nature of M. Aurelius's writings; they do not entitle him to a high place among literary men, but they show that his personal character was singularly sound and noble.

M. Cornelius Fronto held the position of tutor to M. Aurelius, and many letters of his are preserved which exhibit a feeling of strong affection for his pupil[6]. It must have been a great blow to Fronto when M. Aurelius gave up rhetoric for the study of philosophy. Fronto writes fairly good Latin in a somewhat pedantic vein, and shows a considerable acquaintance with past events[7]. But his knowledge is not permeated by that quickening spirit which changes pedantry into enlightenment and puts flesh upon the dry bones of

---

[1] M. Aur. εἰς ἑαυτ. 1, 16.   [2] Ib. id. 5, 27; 6, 3; 6, 2; 9, 1; 9. 4.
[3] Ib. id. 5, 16.   [4] Ib. id. 6, 30.   [5] Ib. id. 8, 30.
[6] M. Corn. Fronto, ad M. Caes. et invicem.   [7] Principia Historiae.

miscellaneous information. He was a rhetorician and grammarian, and discusses minute points with regard to the formation of words, but he shows very little care in his writings to his pupil what that pupil might put for the matter of his speech, provided only that the style were such as would satisfy that itching propensity for strange and affected diction, which was one of the worst characteristics of the literature of the times.

For the rest of the literary life of the period reference may be made to the *Noctes Atticae* of *Aulus Gellius*. Gellius was apparently a native of Rome, but resided at Athens, where he met from time to time Fronto, Herodes Atticus, Favorinus, Sex. Caecilius, and other men of letters. His *Noctes Atticae* contain a vast fund of miscellaneous information and many extracts from otherwise unknown writers, but the work is spoilt by the same affectation which characterizes Apuleius—the desire for strange words. Gellius gives many pleasant pictures of the life and intellectual conversation enjoyed by various persons in Athens under the auspices of Herodes Atticus, the rich and liberal patron of arts. Those Romans who were in Athens studying the Greek arts loved to congregate at the house of Herodes and discuss there knotty points of antiquarian lore[1]. Or again, the passionate Favorinus might be paying a visit from Ephesus to Athens[2], having left behind him his rivalry with the rugged orator Polemon of Smyrna, and he would take the opportunity of ridiculing the unwarrantable derivations of words in which the grammarians delighted, or of

[1] Gellius, *Noct. Att.* i. 2; xviii. 2.
[2] Philostr. *V. Soph.* i. 8; i. 25.

deciding some difficult point of law for Aulus Gellius[1]. All such discussions Gellius took care to record; for it was in such trivial matters that he found himself most at home.

However, it is not to Aulus Gellius alone that the epithet "trivial" must be applied; it is needed for the description of the literature of the period as a whole. Much there is in the literature of the reign of Antoninus Pius which may interest or amuse; some things there are which may even be called brilliant; but the verdict on the literature of the reign must be that the matter of it is trivial and trivially handled. Many men wrote, and wrote respectably, but they did nothing more than dabble on the outskirts of literature, pleasing themselves, no doubt, and at times pleasing their readers, but always failing in matter or in style to reach the heights of true literary merit.

[1] Gellius, *Noct. Att.* iii. 18.

CHAPTER VI.

Religion.

MANY and varied were the religions which appealed to the different sections of the Roman world when Antoninus Pius took up the reins of Empire, and, although his accession was not marked by any decisive change of policy towards religious bodies, his personal character and his private inclinations were not without their effect on the position of the various beliefs. Antoninus Pius himself was earnest, thoughtful and conscientious, severe yet full of kindly feeling, self-restrained, weighty and sober[1]; and he seems to have impressed his character not on the minds of M. Aurelius and his immediate associates alone, but on the whole thought and feeling of his Empire. He was an Emperor who never failed to conduct the customary sacrifices in person, unless serious illness prevented him[2], and an inscription was set up in his honour by the Senate and People of Rome in the following terms:—"S. P. Q. R. optimo maximoque principi et cum summa benignitate iustissimo ob insignem erga caerimonias publicas curam ac religionem[3]." And again, at Delphi a dedication[4]—dated 150 A.D.—was made in honour of Antoninus Pius

---

[1] Cf. chap. v. § 1.
[2] *V. P.* 11, 3.
[3] *C. I. L.* vi. 1001.
[4] *Inscr. Graec. Sic. et Ital.* 1050.

and his family by the Delphians in memory of his dutiful services to the God and his benefactions to the town of Delphi. We may infer then that Antoninus Pius was making some effort to infuse new life into the effete ceremonies of Roman worship, and that by his own diligent attention to religious duties he was endeavouring to spread a religious spirit throughout the Empire.

The religious revival which was set on foot at this time was directed towards the awakening of the old republican spirit of reverence for the gods of Greek and Roman mythology. It was the natural direction in which a religious revival instigated by Antoninus Pius would operate; for the whole tendency of Antoninus's reign was to revert as far as possible to republican forms and to revive the simpler tastes of early Rome. Moreover the fact that the 900th anniversary of the founding of Rome fell in the year 147 A.D. was an additional circumstance which turned men's attention towards the religious beliefs of the early Republic.

Throughout the reign coins were struck which bore devices illustrative of the early mythology and more especially of the doings of Hercules in Italy. The following types[1] will serve to show the character of these coins:—

140—143 A.D. { O = Antoninus Aug. Pius P. P. Tr. P. Cos. III.
R = (Hercules has just conquered Cacus, cf. Ov. *Ff.* I. 552).

155 A.D. { O = Antoninus Aug. Pius P. P. Tr. P. XVIII.
R = (Hercules sacrifices after conquering Cacus, cf. Ov. *Ff.* I. 579).

[1] Eckhel, *Doct. numm.* vol. 7, pp. 29—35.

RELIGION. 143

{ O = Antoninus Aug. Pius P. P. Tr. P. Cos. IIII.
R = (Hercules feasts after sacrifice, cf. Verg. *Aen.* 8, 269). (This third coin should be dated to 145—147 A.D. because Cos. IIII = 145 A.D. and after 147 A.D. Tr. Pot. is followed by a number on coins.)

Again, on coins of 140—143 A.D. Hercules is seen in the garden of the Hesperides, on coins of 145—147 A.D. he is represented at the moment of his discovery of Telephus, while a coin of 148 A.D. pictures him in combat with the Centaurs. Nor were the other figures of Roman mythology neglected. Jupiter is shown on coins (157 A.D.) triumphing over the giants; Vulcan (159 A.D.) is seen at his forge, while Minerva watches his work; Diana appears (140—143 A.D.) riding with a torch in her hand; Prometheus (140—143 A.D.) is depicted in the act of fashioning man, and Mars (140—143 A.D.) is seen with spear and shield hovering in the air over the sleeping Rhea[1]. The heroes, too, of Roman legend or history are shown on coins. Aeneas (145—147 A.D.) with Anchises on his shoulders leads Ascanius by the hand, or stops to gaze upon the sow and her litter. The she-wolf is seen suckling Romulus and Remus, while the Augur Navius (140—143 A.D.) appears in the act of cutting the whetstone, and Horatius Cocles (140—143 A.D.) swimming the Tiber after his memorable conflict.

In 140—143 A.D. a coin of the following type was struck in honour of Aesculapius:—

{ O = Antoninus Aug. Pius P. P. Tr. P. Cos. III.
R = Aesculapius. (Two arches in a river, from one of which projects the prow of a ship, on which is a serpent. Near sits a native on the ground holding a reed. Behind is a building.)

[1] Cf. Juv. xi. 107 "pendentisque dei" (applied to Mars).

This coin must be connected with the visit of Aesculapius to Rome in 290 B.C., when he was summoned from Epidaurus to remove a pestilence. Coming on a trireme in form of a serpent he landed on the island in the Tiber, and a temple was set up to him at the place of his disembarkation. Another coin of 145 —147 A.D. represents Aesculapius sitting at an altar with a dog at his feet—a reference to the legend that when he was exposed by his mother he was guarded by a dog[1].

By coins a spirit of interest in the old mythology was fostered, and other means to the same end were also tried. In honour of Aesculapius and kindred gods Antoninus built or restored several structures in the neighbourhood of Epidaurus[2]; and his example was followed in other parts of Greece by the liberal Herodes Atticus. This free-handed benefactor built at Agrae in Attica[3] a large temple in honour of Artemis Agrotera, using costly Pentelic marble for its construction; at Olympia[4] he used the same material for new statues of Demeter and Corè to replace the older figures, and again at Delphi[5] he substituted Pentelic marble for the native stone in the stadium, that the games of the Delphian god might be solemnized

---

[1] Paus. 2, 26 and 27.

[2] Paus. 2, 27, 7, Antonius's buildings near Epidaurus were:—
    (i)   Bath of Aesculapius.
    (ii)   Temple to θεοί ἐπιδῶται.
    (iii) Temple to Hygeia, Aesculapius and Apollo.
    (iv) Restoration of Porch of Cotys.
    (v)   Roofing of old temple of Aesculapius.
    (vi) Reservoirs and minor improvements.

[3] Paus. 1, 19, 7.   [4] Paus. 6, 21, 2.   [5] Paus. 10, 32, 1.

amid befitting surroundings. Poseidon too received at Corinth[1] an offering from Herodes, which consisted of four horses in gold, with ivory trappings, attended by two Tritons and drawing figures of Amphitrite, Poseidon and Palaemon, all in gold and ivory. Again, at various places in or near Rome, shrines and chapels were set up in honour of the old gods; in 139 A.D. a temple[2] shared by Jupiter, Juno and Minerva was restored; in 141 A.D. and again in 149 A.D. dedications[3] were made to Silvanus; in 148 A.D. a shrine[4] was set up in honour of Jupiter, and another in 157 A.D. with this inscription:—"Iovi custodi et genio thesaurorum aram C. Iulius Augusti libertus d. d. dedicavit XIII. K. Febr. M. Civica Barbaro M. Metilio Cos.[5]"; while Hercules the Preserver received an altar in 159 A.D.[6] Nor were the minor deities neglected, for in 160 A.D.[7] a centurion of Legio VII. Gemina made a dedication in honour of "Suleviae et Campestres."

Moreover such time-honoured religious corporations as the Fratres Arvales[8] were encouraged and brought into special prominence in Pius's reign. It may of course be a purely accidental circumstance that some of the most important inscriptions relating to the Arvals belong to the reign of Antoninus Pius, but it seems probable that the existence of these inscriptions is due to the fact that the records of the acts of the Arvals were especially carefully kept at this time, and that their doings were regarded as matters of considerable

---

[1] Paus. 2, 1, 7.   [2] C. I. L. vi. 401.   [3] C. I. L. vi. 635, 644.
[4] C. I. L. vi. 375.   [5] C. I. L. vi. 376.   [6] C. I. L. vi. 307.
[7] C. I. L. vi. 768.
[8] Cf. G. Boissier, *La Religion Romaine*, I. 362—373.

importance. At least M. Aurelius Caesar was Master of the body in 145 A.D.[1] and his tenure of that office cannot have failed to increase the *prestige* of the Fratres Arvales. For the year 155 A.D. an incomplete but fairly extensive record of the doings of the Arvals has been preserved, which it may be interesting to give in this place[2]:—

January 3. Meeting on the Capitol for taking vows on behalf of the Emperor's safety. In the absence of the Master Avillius Quadratus, M. Fulvius Apronianus presided as *pro magistro*, and among those present were M. Valerius Homullus and C. Iulius Maximus.

January 7. Meeting in the ante-chapel of the Temple of Concord under the presidency of C. Iulius Maximus. The days May 17, 19 and 20 were fixed for the celebration of a sacrifice to Dea Dia and the offering of prayers for the safety of the Emperor, M. Aurelius, the Imperial family, the Senate, the people and the Arvals.

May 17. Double sacrifice by Arvals:—first of incense and wine; and next a similar sacrifice, while all lay on white couches. Boys, whose fathers and mothers were still alive, and who were the sons of senators, assisted in the sacrifice.

May 19. Sacrifice in the grove of Dea Dia,—two sows and a white cow offered. A feast followed, after which came a procession with garlands. Next a fat lamb was sacrificed and incense and wine were offered. Then Statius Cassius Taurinus was elected Master for 156 A.D. with Antoninus Pius himself as flamen. A feast was then held in the house of Avillius Quadratus, which was followed by chariot-races.

May 20. Supper. Offerings of incense, wine and fruits.

May 30. Sow and lamb offered for the expiation of the fall of a tree.

[1] *C. I. L.* vi. 2085.

[2] *C. I. L.* vi. 2086. *C. I. L.* vi. 2084, gives a shorter but similar account for 139 A.D., and from a comparison it appears that festivals and more important meetings occurred on certain fixed days each year.

Such was the activity of the Arvals during the reign of Antoninus Pius. If we remember at the same time how careful the Emperor was for the due observance of all ceremonies, and how anxious he was to bring the figures of the old mythology before the eyes of his subjects, it is impossible not to see that he was endeavouring to give life again to the old dead worship of Jupiter and his fellow-deities and to bring into fashion once more the religion of the early Republic.

But the attempt was doomed to failure from the beginning. A hard, practical, incoherent religion may suffice for a struggling warrior race; but when that race has reaped the reward of its struggles in the possession of peace and prosperity, it needs a religion which will on the one hand excite some enthusiasm or on the other bear a calm inspection. There was nothing in the sternly practical religion of early Rome which could appeal to the imagination of thinking men; there was nothing deep enough in it to stand the test of a leisurely examination. It could not be adopted in the reign of Antoninus Pius, and the educated were forced to look elsewhere for a plausible conception of the supernatural.

Many turned towards the frenzied religions of the East, and some of these sought satisfaction in the worship of Magna Mater[1]. Others found what they wanted in the worship of Mithras, the Persian Sun-god, whose

---

[1] Cf. Schiller, *Röm. Kais.* ii. 681, and Friedländer, *Darstell.* 3^b. 502. Taurobolia and Criobolia were just coming into favour. Cf. Wilmanns, 119. We find these sacrifices at a slightly later period in connection with the worship of Attis, Minerva Berecyntia and Magna Mater at Beneventum. *C. I. L.* ix. 1538 and 1540.

cult was now beginning to spread over the greater part of the Roman Empire[1]. At Grumentum an inscription[2] was set up in honour of Mithras, the unconquered Sun-god, and similar inscriptions are found at Puteoli, Interamna, Ferentinum, Thermae Himeraeae, and numerous places throughout Italy and the provinces[3]. At Naples an inscription[4] of this nature is accompanied by a design representing a naked man drawing a bull from a cave, with fasces and torches at hand—a design which apparently symbolizes the victory of the Sun over the powers of Darkness. Other foreign worships which had a hold on Roman minds were the cults of Isis and Sarapis. The cult of Isis had maintained a footing in Rome in spite of repeated attempts to expel it[5], and now a devotee even erected a statue of Isis in Alexandria for the safety of Antoninus Pius himself[6]. The worship of Sarapis was firmly established in Italy. At Praeneste[7] a lustral vase has been found, used at that city in 157 A.D. in the worship of Sarapis, and another inscription of 157 A.D. refers to a temple of Sarapis erected by C. Valerius Hermaiscus to Διὶ Ἡλίῳ μεγάλῳ Σαραπίδι καὶ τοῖς συννάοις Θεοῖς[8]; while in Rome itself there was a large sect of the worshippers of Sarapis, with a prophet named Embes at their head[9].

Of the Imperial cult itself there is no need to speak at length, since Antoninus Pius was not conspicuous for

[1] Cf. G. Boissier, *La Religion Romaine*, i. 412—413.
[2] *C. I. L.* x. 204.   [3] *C. I. L.* x. 1591, 5331, 5827, 7337.
[4] *C. I. L.* x. 1479.
[5] Tert. *Apol.* 6.   Dio Cass. xl. 47, xlii. 26, liii. 2.   Val. Max. i. iii. 3. Tac. *Hist.* 3. 74.   Suet. *Dom.* 1.
[6] *C. I. G.* 4683 b.   [7] *C. I. L.* xiv. 2904.
[8] *Inscr. Graec. Sic. et Ital.* 1127.   [9] *I. G. S. et I.* 1084.

his connection with this branch of religion. He was indeed energetic in his efforts to procure the canonization of Hadrian[1], but this was perhaps from motives of policy, or at most of filial affection, rather than from those of religion. He also built a temple to Hadrian, and instituted Hadrianales for his worship, but beyond these by no means unusual signs of adherence to the worship of Emperors[2] little is known. The truth is that this cult had now reached its highest possible development. It had spread throughout the Empire and could spread no further, but it was not the religion to take a strong hold of any man.

There were three classes of heathen religions before men's eyes:—first, the old Roman worship, which Antoninus was endeavouring to revive, but which under the existing conditions of Roman life could never regain its lost ground; next, the enthusiastic religions of the East, which could attract for the moment, but whose deceits and absurdities would never hold men for long; lastly, the Imperial cult, with no pretensions to deep thought and feeling, which had already reached its highest possible development.

In these three classes of religion there was not one which could be expected to have a great future before it. It is now left for us to enquire into the relations of the Emperor and of the Empire with a particular religion, which was undoubtedly gaining ground and was already making its voice heard in the palace itself —the religion of the Christians. But before we can

[1] *V. P.* 5, 1 and 2; 8, 2.
[2] Cf. for political importance of this cult, G. Boissier, *La Religion Romaine*, 1. 79 and 105.

start upon this enquiry it will be necessary for the better understanding of the subject to go back some distance, and to give a short sketch of the history of Christianity in its relations with the earlier Emperors and with all classes of Roman society. For we shall find that the attitude of the Imperial government to Christianity was legally the same throughout the century 60 A.D.—160 A.D., and that the position of the Christians during this period was theoretically unchanged, whatever the variations in their actual condition, owing to the temperament or necessities of individual Emperors or Legati[1].

It was an old principle of Roman policy that no god was to be consecrated[2] without the sanction of the Senate. Religion had been always closely interwoven with the political activity of Rome, and he who did not worship Rome's gods, or who worshipped strange gods, was guilty of treason against the State. However, as Rome extended her power, first over Italy and the adjacent islands, and then far to the East and West, she came into contact with states possessing national religions of their own. With the wisdom characteristic of her behaviour towards subject nations she allowed these states to retain their national worship, and in part assimilated the new deities with her own[3]. Thus for political reasons many new gods were recognized.

[1] The following account of the relations of Christianity to the Roman government down to 138 A.D. is not intended as a historical narrative of incidents. Only so much incident has been included as seemed necessary for the clear understanding of the tendencies of each reign. But even then I have found it necessary to extend the limits of the space which I had allotted to the investigation.

[2] Tert. *Apol.* 5. [3] Cf. Livy, *passim*.

Others were not definitely recognized, but were tolerated so long as their worship was not subversive to the Roman morality and religion¹; and the police were entrusted with the duty of interfering, when the limits imposed by Roman morality and religion were passed².

With the progress of civilization and the growth of the thousand new conditions which mark a mighty Empire as distinct from a struggling warrior state, the old religion of Rome, with its cold-blooded bargaining between God and man, was found insufficient³, and the educated turned to cults which appealed to the emotional side of human nature. It has been shown that the authorities endeavoured to keep such cults within narrow limits. They stripped the Eastern frenzied worship of Magna Mater of its more objectionable features, while they partially suppressed the Bacchanals, with their midnight revels and their vast suspected organization. Yet they could not remove the tendency towards new religions of the enthusiastic type; and in spite of repeated prohibitions the worship of the Egyptian Isis obtained a sure footing in Rome and flourished throughout the first three centuries of the Empire⁴. In truth only intolerant creeds were suppressed, or those which were dangerous to the morality, order or unity of the Empire; such as Druidism, which was suppressed by Claudius, owing to its exclusively national character

---

[1] Cf. Hardy, *Christianity and Rom. Gov.* p. 7.
[2] Liv. 4. 30 (425 B.C.), 25. 1 (213 B.C.); cf. stripping of worship of Magna Mater of objectionable features Dionys. 2. 19; cf. suppression of Bacchanals (188 B.C.) Liv. 39. 8, sqq.
[3] Cf. G. Boissier, *La Religion Romaine*, I. 383—394.
[4] Tert. *Apol.* 6; Dio Cass. xl. 47, liii. 2; Tac. *Hist.* 3. 74, etc.

and to the objectionable practice of human sacrifice which was involved in its ritual[1].

The Roman government was first brought into real contact with the Jews by the conquests of Cn. Pompeius Magnus in the East. It found them to be a nation[2], possessed indeed of an intolerant and exclusive religion, but scattered throughout the world and linked together not in a mainly local or political unity, but chiefly by the bonds of a common theocracy. It seemed then that no political danger could be expected from the Jewish religion, and toleration was readily granted to the Jews. Subsequently—as a reward for the friendship of Herod —Augustus granted to the Jews exceptional privileges[3]. Besides the free enjoyment of their religion they were allowed exemption from objectionable duties, such as taking the military *sacramentum* and performing civil or military tasks on the Sabbath; their συναγωγαί were exempted from the general law against *collegia*, and they were allowed a certain jurisdiction over their own members. There was indeed no middle course between protection and persecution in dealing with the religion of an obstinate and energetic nation such as the Jews, whose whole life centred round their religion. But there was a difference between the Eastern Jews, who were still a nation, and the Jews who had settled in the West and had in some cases become Roman citizens. The former might be a source of anxiety unless treated with exceptional favour, the latter were isolated and too weak to command favourable treatment. Tiberius

---

[1] Pliny, *H. N.* 30. 1, 13.
[2] Cf. Hardy, *Christianity and Rom. Gov.* p. 20.
[3] Joseph. *Ant. Iud.* xiv. 10, §§ 6, 12, 17.

therefore, while leaving the Eastern Jews unmolested, persecuted those who had become Roman citizens, arguing that the enjoyment of citizenship was inconsistent with the enjoyment of specially Jewish privileges[1]. Gaius followed in the footsteps of Tiberius, and even went so far as to interfere with the privileges of the Eastern Jews. But the persecution raised too great a storm, and the Jews were for some years left alone[2]. Their privileged position was, however, too exceptional to be free from danger. Mismanagement on the part of the Imperial procurator and foolish counsels among the Jewish leaders led to the destruction of Jerusalem and the annihilation of the national existence of the Jews in 71 A.D. Henceforward Judaism was tolerated as a *religio licita*, and its members were required to attach themselves to one synagogue, to enter their names as Jews on lists kept by the Roman police and to pay a tax of two drachmas[3]. Thus politically the Jews ceased to exist, but their religion was most carefully protected[4] by the government, a protection which was all the more needed, since the character and habits of the Jews were already earning them the hatred of the educated classes of the Empire[5].

Christianity was at first considered to be a variety of Judaism even by the Jews themselves. The earliest converts continued to worship in the Temple[6], and the

[1] Tac. *Ann.* ii. 85.   [2] Philo, *Leg. ad Gaium*, p. 1019.

[3] Momms. *Hist. Zeit.* lxiv. p. 425; Joseph. *Bell. Iud.* vii. 6, 6; Dio C. 66, 7; Suet. *Dom.* 12.

[4] Cod. Theod. 16. 8, 9.

[5] Pliny, *H. N.* 13, 4; Quint. *Inst. Or.* iii. 7, 21; Juv. 14, 100; Tac. *Hist.* v. 2—5.

[6] Acts ii. 46.

earliest preaching of the Apostles was directed towards Jews only[1]; the Jewish authorities proscribed the new religion as a Jewish heresy[2], the Jews alone were the early persecutors, and the Roman authorities were unwilling to interfere in what they regarded as merely sectarian differences[3]. But by degrees the name Χριστιανοὶ became familiar to Eastern ears and to the ears of the Roman officials, coupled with charges of disloyalty and seditious conduct, which St. Paul was careful to deny[4]. Moreover the Gentile Christians soon outnumbered the Jewish Christians[5]; for while Judaism had incidentally attracted outsiders, it was the end and aim of Christianity to do so[6]. It must therefore have been apparent to the Eastern world at an early date that Christianity was in its essence a new movement; and it would seem a movement of some political importance, since it consisted in the worship of a Person who had lately lived on the earth, and was thus in a manner a rival of the worship of Emperors.

But it was as a social movement that Christianity aroused the greatest opposition[7]. It was a movement which interfered with the conditions of society, with family life, popular amusements and the ordinary religious observances, which rebuked the lax morality of the times, and even menaced various trade interests. It raised the lower classes to an equality with the rich, promising them happiness in a future world to com-

---

[1] Acts xi. 19.   [2] Acts iv. 18; v. 28; vii. 58; viii. 3; xxv. 8.
[3] Acts xviii. 14, 15; xxiv., xxv. 14 sqq.   [4] Acts xxv. 8; xvii. 7.
[5] Acts xiii. 47; xviii. 6.
[6] Tac. *H.* v. 5; cf. Friedländer, *Darstell.* 1, 502, and 3, 610.
[7] Cf. Hardy, *op. cit.* pp. 45—53.

pensate for their disadvantages in the present. It caused a reckless disregard for business and the ordinary duties of life—for why should a man go through the routine of commercial life, when the end of the world was shortly to come? It created divisions in families and endangered the ancestral cults of each house, while at times the property of a family would be transferred to Christian funds, or a daughter would be persuaded to resist the matrimonial projects of her parents[1], or again, a household might be set by the ears through some proselytizing Christian slave. Besides this, Christians steadily refused to take part in the public festivals with their praise of heathen gods, or to attend games with their sacrifice of human or animal life. They would not take the oath in court, they objected to service in the army, and avoided the honours and obligations of civic office. Last, but not least, Christianity interfered with trade. At Philippi[2] great excitement was caused by the curing of a mad soothsayer, from whom her masters had derived considerable profit. At Ephesus[3] the metalworkers saw that their hope of gain would be lost if the worship of Christ succeeded that of Artemis; while at a subsequent period Christianity ruined for a time the dealers in fodder for sacrificial animals in Asia[4]. Christianity indeed seemed to be opposed to the customs and life of the Roman Empire at every turn. It professed to be a disintegrating religion and to be outside the world[5]. It is not then to be wondered if Christians came to be regarded as the natural enemies of the

[1] Cf. Paul and Thekla. [2] Acts xvi. 20.
[3] Acts xix. 23. [4] Pliny-Trajan, *Ep.* 96, § 10.
[5] St. Luke xxi. 16; Just. *Apol.* 1, 11.

world at large, and if "hostile odium" or "odium humani generis" were regarded as the essential characteristics of Christianity. But the populace went a step further. They had come to the conclusion that Christianity involved in itself a hatred of the human race, and it was not long before they interpreted this hatred to mean among other things the defiance of every moral law and the commission of every variety of abominable crime[1]. They found some support for their charges in the private assemblies of Christians, which by analogy with the orgies of Oriental cults were regarded as the hotbeds of immorality and corruption.

In Rome itself we find that the Christians were regarded as a sect of the Jews by the Roman government during the reign of Claudius[2]. Suetonius says of Claudius that "Iudaeos impulsore Chresto assidue tumultuantes Roma expulit"—a remark which can only mean that quarrels arose between Jews and Christians, and that the Roman magistrates did not deign to interfere in what they considered a sectarian dispute, but solved the difficulty by banishing from Rome both parties, as they thought, under the name of Jews. But the Gentile Christians would not be affected by this measure, and it was as a Gentile and not a Jewish body that the Christians spread in Rome[3]. In 57 A.D. a noble Roman lady, Pomponia Graecina[4], was accused "superstitionis externae rea" and handed over to the domestic

[1] Tac. *Ann.* xv. 44, etc.
[2] Dio C. 60, 6; Suet. *Claud.* 25. Suetonius himself probably only affects ignorance of the distinction; but if he is at all trustworthy, Claudius must have regarded Christians and Jews as not really different.
[3] Hardy, *op. cit.* pp. 55, 56. [4] Tac. *Ann.* xiii. 32.

tribunal of her family, to be dealt with on account of her "continua tristitia," "cultus lugubris," "non animus nisi moestus":—charges which seem to point to her Christianity. And in face of the fact that Pomponius Graecinus[1], in the 2nd century A.D., was undoubtedly a Christian, there need be little hesitation in ranking this Pomponia Graecina as a Christian also. We may conclude that during the two years' undisturbed preaching of St. Paul in Rome[2] a few years later Christianity was continually spreading among the non-Jewish inhabitants of Rome, unmolested by any definite State persecution.

But from this extension of Christianity among the Gentiles it must soon have become apparent to the magistrates in Rome that Jews and Christians were two distinct bodies, while it cannot be doubted that the Emperor received from time to time reports from provincial governors[3] in the East, referring to the Christians as a distinct sect—for they were well known as such throughout the provinces of Syria, Asia and Galatia[4]. Hence we may affirm that Christians were known in Rome to be distinct from Jews by about 60 A.D., and it was not long before they suffered persecution as a distinct sect.

The persecution of the Christians by Nero is a point that needs to be most clearly understood before any accurate idea can be formed of the subsequent position of the Christians under the Roman Empire. It was not, indeed, a persecution by religious fanatics directed

---

[1] De Rossi, *Rom. Sott.* 2, 364.
[2] Acts xxviii. 30.   [3] Hardy, p. 63.
[4] Ramsay, *The Church in the Rom. Empire*, pp. 56, 57. Acts xi. 26.

against a sect, whose tenets were objected to on religious grounds, but it was none the less a persecution, for what Pliny[1] subsequently called "nomen ipsum" and not a mere attack on the "flagitia cohaerentia nomini." In fact at this time there was no distinction drawn either by the Roman government or the Roman populace between the two. It has been shown that Christianity seemed to a certain extent politically dangerous, with its utter disregard for nationality and social position and its characteristic *obstinatio*[1]; that it interfered with the existing conditions of society at every turn; and that Christians were suspected of gross immorality. Hence the populace came to the conclusion that all these things were the inevitable concomitants of Christianity and its characteristic marks. They united them all under the name of "odium humani generis," and believed that this hatred of mankind was the actual religion of Christianity[2],—a belief to which they were perhaps led by the false representations of the Jews. In proof of this identification of Christianity with "odium humani generis" by the Roman people, several passages may be quoted. Tacitus[3] speaks of men "quos per flagitia invisos vulgus Christianos appellabat," thus coupling the bestowal of the name with the belief in the crimes of Christianity; in the same passage he speaks of Christianity as "exitiabilis superstitio." A few lines further on he says, "per urbem etiam...(erumpebat)...quo cuncta undique atrocia aut pudenda confluunt celebranturque," clearly showing that Christianity was itself regarded as "atrox" and "pudenda," i.e. as in-

[1] Pliny-Traj. *Ep.* 96.   [2] Tert. *Apol.* 21.
[3] Tac. *Ann.* xv. 44.

volving the moral and other crimes charged against it. Again Tacitus says, "correpti qui fatebantur," which can only mean that confession of Christianity was immediately followed by arrest, while he adds that those who confessed their Christianity or were denounced as Christians were punished not so much "in crimine incendii quam odio humani generis,"—a fact which is additional evidence of the identification of Christianity with hatred of mankind. Again, Suetonius[1] calls the Christians "genus hominum superstitionis novae ac maleficae," a new and malicious superstition, i.e. one which manifested malice or hatred of the human race. It is true that Tacitus and Suetonius wrote at a considerable distance of time from the events which they were describing, but in the present case that fact is no argument against the view set forth here—that Christianity at this time was itself considered equivalent to hatred of mankind. If this seemed to educated Romans to be the character of Christianity, after it had been known for 70 or 80 years, much more would this have been the case when the religion was presented for the first time in a rough and perhaps not altogether judicious manner to the gaze of the ignorant and turbulent Roman mob.

It seems impossible to believe that the Neronian persecution was anything else than a persecution of the "nomen ipsum" of Christianity. Christianity was thought to involve essentially "odium humani generis" with its accompanying crimes. Consequently, as soon as the Christianity of a man was established,

---

[1] Suet. *Nero*, 16.

his moral, social and political crimes were established in the eyes of the crowd, and he was therefore worthy of death.

The actual occasion of the Neronian persecution was the Fire of Rome. Nero could not convince the Roman populace that the Fire was not due to his orders, and he therefore endeavoured to bring into prominence the hated sect of Christians[1], hoping thereby that the populace would give vent to its indignation by attacking the Christians and not himself. But it appears from Tacitus that his device was seen through, and, though the populace was ready to persecute the Christians, yet it considered them guilty only of general "odium humani generis," and not of the special act of incendiarism. In fact Nero's cruelties in the end disgusted even the Roman populace, and a reaction set in. Pity was felt for the Christians, who were regarded at last not as criminals suffering merited punishment, but as victims of a monster's cruelty. And it was this change in popular feeling which procured the Christians comparative freedom from persecution for the next twenty years.

In its legal aspect the persecution of Christianity under Nero as well as under subsequent Emperors was a matter which lay in the hands of the police. Christianity was not a "religio licita," but theoretically was the object of a standing persecution[2], though this persecution might in practice be dropt from time to time. We have already seen how the police interfered under

[1] Tac. *Ann.* xv. 44; Euseb. *H. E.* ii. 25; Sulp. Severus, *Chron.* 2, 29.
[2] Momms. *Röm. Gesch.* v. 523 n.

the Republic to check or to suppress various religions, which appeared subversive to order or morality, and their action was exactly the same with regard to Christianity under the Empire[1]. Legally the Christians were as liable to punishment as brigands or other criminals; but practically, if they could avoid coming into contact with Roman officials or avoid exciting an outbreak of popular hostility, the Roman police were content to let matters slide. And this was the case not only in Rome but throughout the Empire. However, if the Emperor or his representatives in the provinces insisted on the strict observance of Imperial religion, or if popular feeling were excited against Christianity, or if in any way the Christians became prominent, there was only one possible course;—on proof of a man's Christianity, he must be summarily sentenced by the governor in the provinces, by the *praef. urbi*, or the Emperor in Rome.

Under Vespasian and Titus the Christians were probably left undisturbed[2], for no record exists of persecution during the reigns of these Emperors. The populace had not recovered from the reaction caused by Nero's cruelties, while the Flavian dynasty was too busily occupied with the work of government to turn its attention to the religion of a humble sect. But with Domitian, the last of the dynasty, the existing policy of oppression was again put into operation. Domitian himself was a determined supporter of the worship of Emperors, and his orders were often issued under the

[1] Cf. Suet. *Nero*, 16, which includes the persecution of Christians among a number of other police regulations carried out under Nero.

[2] Euseb. *H. E.* iii. 17.

style, "Deus et Dominus noster hoc fieri iubet¹." Moreover the disturbances of his time caused the populace to look about once more for some object on which to vent its discontent; and finally the suspicious nature of the Flavian dynasty², its fear of political rivals, found its greatest development in Domitian. From a combination of these causes the machinery of persecution was once more set in motion, and Jews and Christians alike suffered³. The persecution seems to have begun with an attempt to enforce the payment of the Jewish tribute of two drachmas from those who had in accordance with a fashionable craze adopted various habits of Jewish life⁴, and from those Jews who had become Christians. Dio Cassius says that the persecution was directed only against those who were found to be ἐς τὰ τῶν Ἰουδαίων ἤθη ἐξοκέλλοντες⁵, but in the face of the evidence of Eusebius and Sulpicius Severus we must infer⁶ that Dio Cassius is in error either from carelessness or from the literary affectation of complete ignorance concerning Christians⁷. Dio Cassius says that among many others Flavius Clemens (cos. 95 A.D.), cousin of Domitian, and his wife Domitilla—also related to Domitian—were tried on the charge of ἀθεότης and were put to death, but Eusebius⁸ is probably right in saying that the woman was banished and not put to death. It is worthy of note that this Flavius Clemens,

---

¹ Suet. *Dom.* 13; Schiller, *Röm. Kais*, 1, 536.
² Suet. *Vesp.* 15; Suet. *Dom. passim*.
³ Euseb. *H. E.* iii. 17—19.   ⁴ Suet. *Dom.* 12; cf. Juv. xiv. 100.
⁵ Dio Cass. lxvii. 14.   ⁶ Euseb. *l.c.*, Sulp. Sev. *Chron.* 2, 31.
⁷ Cf. Aristides (Dind.), 2, 402, who refers to "those impious Palestinians"—as if he had no knowledge of them.
⁸ Euseb. *H. E.* iii. 18.

in virtue of his cousinship, was Domitian's nearest relative and might seem in consequence a political rival. Suetonius[1] adds that Acilius Glabrio (cos. 91 A.D.) was prosecuted at the same time as "molitor rerum novarum," a further proof that Domitian had suspicions of political designs in the movement. Eusebius says that Flavia Domitilla was banished for her Christianity[2], and it may not be too much to infer that her husband and Acilius Glabrio were executed as Christians also. Sulpicius Severus[3], who follows Tacitus mainly, may be adduced as additional evidence that Domitian persecuted the Christians as well as the Jews, banishing St. John to Patmos.

It seems then clear enough that there was a Christian persecution under Domitian, but what specially concerns us in it is that the principal sufferers were persons of rank, and that two of them were accused of ἀθεότης and a third as "molitor rerum novarum." It is clear moreover from Dio Cassius's words—ἐπηνέχθη δὲ ἀμφοῖν ἔγκλημα ἀθεότητος, ὑφ' ἧς καὶ ἄλλοι ἐς τὰ τῶν Ἰουδαίων ἤθη ἐξοκέλλοντες κατεδικάσθησαν[4]—that ἀθεότης was the regular charge brought against all the accused in this persecution. We have then to reconcile the charge of ἀθεότης with the charge brought against Acilius Glabrio as "molitor rerum novarum"; for from the evidence adduced it may be reasonably inferred that the offence of Acilius Glabrio was the same as the offence of Flavius Clemens and his companions. Nor have we far to look for such a means of reconciliation. Ἀθεότης was an insult to the majesty of the Emperor by

[1] Suet. *Dom.* 10. [2] Euseb. *H. E.* iii. 18.
[3] Sulp. Sev. *Chron.* 2, 31. [4] Dio Cass. lxvii. 14.

a refusal to participate in the Imperial cult[1]. "Molitor rerum novarum" would then be the name given to the person refusing so to worship, and would be an attempt to explain the reason of his refusal. It implied a similar refusal to worship the Emperor, and it alleged political motives for the refusal. We may then embrace both charges under the name of *Maiestas* and assume that a political bias was given to the charge of Christianity on account of the high position of some of the accused. Accordingly the charge against the Christians was made under the head of *Maiestas*, and Dio Cassius or Xiphilinus—not paying attention to legal accuracy so much as to the general characteristics of the charge—styled the accusation as a refusal to worship Roman gods, i.e. ἀθεότης, while Suetonius, looking at the political importance of the matter, called Acilius Glabrio "molitor rerum novarum."

But though the Christians were now prosecuted under a charge of *Maiestas*, this fact made no practical difference in their position. Mommsen[2] indeed says that, from the first, Christians, when punished for the "nomen ipsum," were punished under the *leges maiestatis*. But it is probable that the procedure during Nero's persecution was very loose and ill-defined, while there were too few, if there were any, cases of persecution during the reigns of Vespasian and Titus to enable us to arrive at a sure conclusion on this point. At any rate, during Domitian's reign and afterwards the attacks on Christians were made under the head of *Maiestas*, and

[1] Cf. G. Boissier, *La Rel. Rom.* i. 79 and 105.
[2] Momms. *Hist. Zeit.* lxiv. p. 396, and *Expositor*, July 1893. Cf. Friedländer, *Darstellungen*, 3, 631.

the proof of Christianity was considered sufficient for a conviction. Now, too, a test of Christianity was introduced[1]—at least we find it freely used in the Eastern provinces a few years later, while even at this date Christians were executed in Asia for refusing to satisfy the test[2]. It was a challenge to those accused of Christianity to swear by the Emperor's genius and to offer incense and wine to his image[3]. Those who refused were by that act guilty of *Maiestas*; but it is not certain that those who complied were immediately liberated. Certainly Pliny[4] did not know what to do with those whom he found to have been Christians and who in his presence complied with the required test. Trajan ordered the release of such prisoners, but the ignorance of Pliny on the point goes to show that till Trajan's time the matter was undecided and probably lay in the discretion of each magistrate.

Accordingly under Domitian Christians were brought within the limits of *Maiestas*; but no new law was passed on the subject, and no change was made in the treatment of Christians except changes in the spirit in which the law was administered, owing to the peculiar character of Domitian. Their religion was still subject to the same police regulations as before, and as before it was the "nomen ipsum" which entailed punishment. The Emperor himself probably tried important person-

---

[1] Pliny-Traj. *Ep.* 96, § 5; Ruinart, *Act. Mart.* p. 696; Revelation xiii. 15; xx. 4.

[2] Asia was specially devoted to Emperor-worship; cf. Tac. *Ann.* iv. 39; Dio Cass. li. 20. So also Domitian; Suet. *Dom.* 13. Hence this seemed a natural test.

[3] Cf. Hardy, *op. cit.* 95—99.   [4] Pliny-Traj. 96, 2, and 97, 2.

ages, such as Flavius Clemens, Domitilla and Acilius Glabrio, but the rank and file of the Christians would come as before into the court of the *praefectus urbi* in Rome or the *legatus* in the provinces. Finally, instead of an ill-defined procedure, a more or less satisfactory test of Christianity had been introduced. But when once the Christianity of a prisoner was established, his condemnation followed immediately, and no proof was required that he was guilty of any other crime.

The persecution of the Christians by Domitian was not of any long duration, nor did any large number of persons suffer under it[1], while a considerable number of those banished by Domitian were subsequently recalled by the same Emperor. After his death there was for some years no general persecution, but riots and consequent attacks on the Christians took place in many districts[2].

Particularly was this the case in the province of Bithynia-Pontus, which in the end became the scene of so general a disturbance that Trajan took the management of it from the Senate and sent C. Plinius Secundus thither as an Imperial *legatus*[3]. It is true that the attacks on the Christians were not the only cause of disorder here, but they were a prominent feature in the disturbances. There had been many Jewish settlers in the district even under the Republic[4], and this fact may have accounted to some extent both for the spread of Christianity there and also for the bitter feelings with which the Christians were there regarded. At any rate there were Christian bishops in the country at an early

[1] Euseb. *H. E.* iii. 20; Tert. *Apol.* 5.   [2] Euseb. *H. E.* iii. 32.
[3] Pliny-Traj. *Ep.* 32, 1 and 34.   [4] Cic. *pro Flacc.* 28.

date and an extensive Christian organization throughout the district[1]. To such a degree had the new religion spread that the heathen temples were deserted and the heathen sacrifices discontinued[2], while the dealers in fodder for sacrificial animals found that in consequence their trade was gone. Trajan, with a view to safeguarding the province, had given Pliny strict orders to suppress all Hetairiai[3], and the Christians as a result of this had discontinued their common meal. But none the less Christianity maintained its hold on urban and rural districts alike, on high and low, young and old, men and women. Orosius[4] says that Trajan first issued a rescript for the execution of all Christians who refused to sacrifice to the Emperor's image, and that Pliny had to point out the vast consequence of this order. But Pliny in his 96th letter recapitulates all the essential facts of the case, and could not have omitted such an important fact as the issuing of this order. Hence we are compelled to disbelieve Orosius's statement.

If we proceed now to examine the 96th letter[5] carefully, we find that the course of Pliny's relations with the Christians was as follows:—

i. The authorities[6] had not made any search for Christians, since it was generally the custom to leave them alone, unless they made themselves unduly prominent or unless a noticeable outburst of popular hatred was directed against them. However, some person or

---

[1] Wiltsch, *Geog. and Statist. of the Church* (transl.), Vol. i. pp. 47—49.
[2] Pliny-Traj. *Ep.* 96, 10. [3] Pliny-Traj. *Ep.* 96, 7; 34.
[4] Orosius, 7, 12. [5] Pliny-Traj. *Ep.* 96. [6] § 2.

168   THE REIGN OF ANTONINUS PIUS.

persons had laid an information against certain individuals as Christians.

ii. Pliny thrice asked the accused[1] whether they were Christians, and, as they all resolutely confessed, he condemned to death those who were provincials, and sent those who were Roman citizens to Rome, to be condemned by the Emperor.

iii. Subsequently an anonymous accusation[2] of Christianity was made against a large number of persons, and Pliny proceeded to try those who were so denounced. Those who at once denied their Christianity and complied with the required tests of worshipping the Emperor and cursing Christ were forthwith liberated[3]. Those who first confessed and then denied their Christianity, or who admitted that they had been, but maintained that they were not now Christians, all eventually complied with the required tests. But Pliny apparently did not liberate them till he had consulted Trajan[4].

So far Pliny had acted in all essential points precisely in accordance with the procedure, which, as we have seen, became customary under Domitian. His plan of asking thrice may have been adopted on his own initiative in order to save the Christians from the consequences of their first confession, while the detention of those who had recanted was an exercise of his discretionary powers and was a severity due to the disturbed state of the province and the numbers of the Christians[5].

[1] §§ 3 and 4.   [2] § 5.
[3] § 6.   [4] § 8.
[5] It was a recognized principle of Roman law that the more numerous the offenders the heavier was the sentence.

But having been sent out under special circumstances Pliny thought it his duty to carry his investigations into Christianity deeper than others had done. The province was disturbed and the marked "obstinatio," which he found in the Christians[1], was exactly the quality which, in the opinion of a governor, would lead to a disturbance. What then was at the bottom of this "obstinatio"? The solution of this question involved an inquiry into the life and habits of the Christians, and from his prisoners Pliny was surprised to learn[2] that the accepted opinion of Christianity as "odium humani generis," with its attendant political, moral, and social crimes, was quite wrong. He found that the only crime of the Christians consisted in meeting on a fixed day before daybreak, honouring Christ as a god with chants and binding themselves to abstain from all manner of crime. After this the Christians had been accustomed to disperse and to meet again later in the day for the enjoyment of an ordinary meal. But this second meeting had been discontinued by the Christians from a desire to avoid offending against Trajan's order concerning Hetairiai or Collegia[3]. In fact, after careful investigation and the examination of two *ancillae* by torture, Pliny considered that there was no danger in Christianity and that it was in no way reprehensible save as a "superstitio prava immodica[4]," i.e. a non-Roman worship of non-Roman gods, which was de-

---

[1] § 3.   [2] § 7.

[3] Cf. Ramsay, *op. cit.* p. 222. The morning meeting was purely religious and so did not break the "collegia" law. The second meeting was a meal (= *sodalitas*) and so came within the law.

[4] § 8.

grading and possibly subversive to the Roman ideal of citizen life[1].

Accordingly Pliny thought that an "obstinatio," which had apparently so little behind it, could be put down by firm and judicious treatment, and he wrote to Trajan[2] that his efforts had already been rewarded by an increased devotion to pagan worship throughout his province and by a renewal of the former sacrifices, which was accompanied by a readier sale of fodder for sacrificial animals. All that was needed, wrote Pliny, was that the hope of pardon should be held out to all who would recant, and then countless numbers of men would return to the worship of the recognized gods.

It now remains for us to consider why Pliny thought it necessary to consult Trajan in this matter, when he himself was already following out correctly a policy which had become customary and well-established. He himself openly gives one reason[3]—namely, the wide extent of Christianity which embraced men, women and children of every rank and station, and had spread through town and country alike. Another fact he puts forward in the words[4], "Cognitionibus de Christianis interfui numquam; ideo nescio quid et quatenus aut puniri soleat aut quaeri." Now it is perfectly possible that Pliny may never have been present at a trial of Christians before he was sent out to the East; but the permanent officials of the province could give him all the information he required[5], and in fact we find him conducting the trials on the prescribed lines. It is

---

[1] Cf. Ramsay, p. 205. [2] § 10.
[3] § 9. Euseb. *H. E.* iii. 33, says this was the reason. [4] § 1.
[5] Cf. Hardy, pp. 106 and 107.

obvious then that while the numbers of the Christians may have been a genuine reason for consulting the Emperor, the plea of ignorance was not. It was a mere excuse and a means of veiling the real motive which prompted Pliny to consult Trajan. The vast extent of Christianity and the new light which had been thrown on its character had made an impression on Pliny, and, without daring to suggest it openly, he desired Trajan to reconsider the whole question of the treatment of the Christians. That this was the motive which induced him to consult Trajan may be seen still more clearly from the nature of the questions which he addresses to that Emperor. He asks:—

1. "Are extenuating circumstances, e.g. age, sex, etc., to be considered[1]?" Now we know that he had hitherto ordered the execution of *all*[2] those Christians who remained resolute. It is plain therefore that the law can have recognized no such extenuating circumstances, and Pliny—a good lawyer—must have known the law. Accordingly his question can only be a hint to Trajan to alter the law.

2. "Is pardon to be granted to those who recant[3]?" It is probable that this was a genuine question. We have seen reason to believe that this point was generally left to the discretion of the magistrate. Pliny thought that Christianity might be stamped out "si sit poenitentiae locus[4]," and he wished the Emperor to make a definite statement in favour of this view.

3. "Haesitavi...an...nomen ipsum, si flagitiis careat, an flagitia cohaerentia nomini puniantur[5]." But Pliny

---

[1] § 2. [2] Cf. § 3. [3] § 2.
[4] Cf. § 10. [5] § 2.

knew that the "nomen ipsum" was a "flagitium" in the eyes of the law and was punishable as such with or without attendant crimes; for he had already administered the law on these lines. His question then can only be a suggestion that instead of Christianity being regarded in itself as "odium humani generis," as a grievous "flagitium," an inquiry should be made in each case as to whether the conduct of the accused was the conduct of a hater of the human race, the conduct of a criminal; that punishment should follow only on the proof of such criminal conduct; in other words that the "nomen ipsum" should go unpunished.

Each one of Pliny's questions is a hint conveyed to Trajan, in as open a manner as the relative positions of the Legate and the Emperor would permit, to authorize the use of milder measures in dealing with the Christians. The answer of the Emperor was in its general effect an authorization of merciful treatment. And the Christians were sensible of this improvement in their position, if we may judge from the statement of Christian historians. Sulpicius Severus[1] says that Trajan "cum tormentis et quaestionibus nihil in Christianos morte aut poena dignum repperisset, saeviri in eos ultra vetuit." Eusebius[2] says that Pliny, alarmed at the numbers of the Christians, consulted Trajan as to what was to be done, showing that Christianity was itself free from crime and in nothing contrary to the law. Trajan's reply was, "τὸ Χριστιανῶν φῦλον μὴ ἐκζητεῖσθαι μὲν, ἐμπεσὸν δὲ κολάζεσθαι," and the effect of this was to moderate persecution, though attacks were still made

---

[1] Sulp. Sev. *Chron.* 2, 31.   [2] Euseb. *H. E.* iii. 33.

by the populace or authorities—ἄνευ προφανῶν διωγμῶν μερικοὺς κατ' ἐπαρχίαν ἐξάπτεσθαι. This shows clearly enough what can be inferred from the words of Trajan's rescript—that the Emperor, while leaning to the side of mercy, did not desire to lay down any hard and fast rules, but only some general principles, and that much still depended on the temper of the provincial governor and the feelings of the provincials themselves. Tertullian[1] corroborates Eusebius, adding that Pliny wrote, "ἐξὼ τοῦ μὴ βούλεσθαι αὐτοὺς εἰδωλολατρεῖν οὐδὲν ἀνόσιον ἐν αὐτοῖς ηὑρηκέναι."

Such were the general characteristics of the views held by Pliny and Trajan concerning the Christians, and of the treatment which was the result of these views. We will now consider the actual reply[2] which Trajan wrote to Pliny. Pliny's questions had not been put in an open fashion, nor are Trajan's answers any more open. Yet it is clear enough that Trajan saw what Pliny's questions meant, for he gives a sufficient answer to each.

1. Pliny had asked, "Are extenuating circumstances, e.g. age, sex, etc., to be considered?" Trajan replied, "Neque enim in universum aliquod, quod quasi certam formam habeat, constitui potest[3]"—showing that he wished the treatment to vary with circumstances, i.e. he ordered his governors to exercise their discretion in taking account of the age, sex, etc. of the Christians, and thus permitted the adoption of more merciful treatment towards certain classes of prisoners.

2. Pliny had asked, "Is pardon to be granted to

---

[1] Tert. *Apol.* 2.   [2] Pliny-Traj. *Ep.* 97.   [3] § 1.

those who recant?" Trajan replied, "Qui negaverit se Christianum esse idque re ipsa manifestum fecerit, id est supplicando diis nostris, quamsi suspectus in praeteritum, veniam ex poenitentia impetret[1]." Thus the answer to Pliny's second question was also merciful.

3. Pliny had asked whether "Nomen ipsum, si flagitiis careat, an flagitia cohaerentia nomini puniantur." Trajan does not answer this question in so many words, but he approves Pliny's past action[2], which had been a punishment of "nomen ipsum," and he adds "si deferantur et arguantur puniendi sunt[3]." He felt himself bound by the Imperial policy handed down without a break from the time of Nero to punish the "nomen ipsum." The principle must be maintained, but Trajan endeavoured to mitigate the severity of its application as far as possible. No effort must be made to seek out Christians, and no account whatever must be taken of an anonymous accusation. In other words the Christians must be undisturbed until some definite accuser came forward and lent his name to a charge against them.

The state religion was part of the Imperial organization[4], and compliance with this religion was expected from all. Hence exception was taken to Christianity *per se*[5], as it involved rejection of the state religion and therein disloyalty to the Imperial government. Accord-

---

[1] § 2. Cf. Min. Fel. *Octav.* 28, "et quasi eierato nomine iam omnia facta sua illa negatione purgaret."

[2] Pliny-Traj. *Ep.* 97, § 1.   [3] § 2.   [4] Tert. *Apol.* 35.

[5] Notable case of persecution for "Nomen" under Trajan:— Ignatius was sent from Syria to Rome and there exposed to beasts, his character being excellent and his only crime his Christianity. Cf. Ignat. *Ep. ad Rom.* 5; Polycarp, *ad Philip.* 9, 13.

ingly Trajan saw that in theory Christianity was dangerous, but practically he knew that it was comparatively harmless, and would be rendered still more so if recantation and secession could be encouraged by merciful means without the surrender of the principle that Christianity was in itself illegal. His reply to Pliny was then a merciful and practical reply, misunderstood by Tertullian, who comments on it in the words, "Negat inquirendos ut innocentes et mandat puniendos ut nocentes[1]." During the succeeding reigns the persecution of Christians was still in theory a standing matter, but it was only applied when popular hatred forced the hands of the governors. And this hatred was due:—(i) to the "Atheism" of Christians, i.e. their refusal to worship the recognized deities; (ii) to their contempt for social enjoyments and their interference with the conditions of trade; (iii) to an unreasoning belief in their moral guilt and in their responsibility for all disasters which might occur[2].

It is not necessary to go any further into the details of the condition of the Christians during Trajan's reign. Enough has been said to show the general features of the treatment which Trajan authorized in dealing with the Christians. And it was on the lines which Trajan laid down that Hadrian and Antoninus Pius regulated their actions in this matter.

During Hadrian's reign a revolt of the Jews broke out in Palestine under the leadership of Barchochebas,

---

[1] Tert. *Apol.* 2.
[2] Cf. Tert. *Apol.* 40, "if the Tiber floods the city, if the Nile will not rise, if rain does not fall, etc., you cry 'Christianos ad leones!'"

who was, according to Eusebius, a mere brigand[1]. His first endeavour had been to unite Jews and Christians against the Roman rule[2], but the Christians had been wise enough to resist his advances and remained loyal to Rome in spite of the persecution and torture with which he tried to force them to revolt[3]. Hadrian suppressed the rebellion in 135 A.D., and then proceeded to Romanize Jerusalem as far as possible[4]. He changed the name of the city to Aelia, forbade the Jews to reside there, and set up heathen temples and statues in the sacred places of the city. Sulpicius Severus[5] says that Hadrian went on to persecute the Christians, but soon stopped, saying that it was unjust to let anyone be tried unless a definite charge were brought against him. We have seen, however, that the Christians remained loyal during the revolt, and Eusebius[6] says that there were no 'state persecutions in Hadrian's reign. Accordingly we may conclude that Severus is wrong—at least in connecting a Christian persecution with the close of the Jewish revolt.

A noticeable point in Hadrian's reign is the appearance of Christian Apologists. The fact of their appearance is more important from our point of view than the matter of their Apologies. It shows that the spirit of No Compromise, which had marked the earlier leaders of Christianity such as Ignatius[7], was giving way before the milder measures now authorized by the Roman

---

[1] Euseb. *H. E.* iv. 6 and 8; Sulp. Sever. *Chron.* 2, 31.
[2] Orosius, 7, 13. [3] Euseb. *H. E.* iv. 8.
[4] Euseb. *H. E.* iv. 6. [5] *Chron.* 2, 31.
[6] Euseb. *H. E.* iv. 7.
[7] Ignat. *Ep. Rom.* 3; *Ep. Ephes.* 12.

government. Ignatius had regarded it as an essential for Christianity that it should be at war with the Roman government, and had considered martyrdom as a thing not only to be endured but to be desired. The Book of Revelation (circ. 95 A.D.) is full of the same spirit[1]; the Roman Emperor is the incarnation of all vice, and his worship is the worship of the Beast[2]. But now that Pliny had endeavoured to get a more correct knowledge of Christianity and had found no crime in it[3], now that Trajan had pronounced in favour of as merciful treatment as possible, there seemed a hope that with fuller knowledge the Emperors might extend a yet wider measure of mercy. It was therefore the business of someone to show that Christianity had no designs against the Imperial government; that it was free from the moral guilt which the populace associated with it; that it was worthy of recognition no less at least than the other foreign worships, which had been admitted into Rome; that it was in no way responsible for the calamities which from time to time might visit the Empire; and that the blame for the disorders arising in various cities rested with the persecutors and not with the Christians. It was to prove these points that the Apologists came forward, Quadratus and Aristides being the leaders. The Apology of Quadratus is unfortunately lost with the exception of brief quotations, but from these it appears that the work was mainly an exposition of Christian beliefs and of no particular historical

---

[1] Cf. Ramsay, *op. cit.* pp. 296—300.
[2] Rev. xiii. 8—15.
[3] Cf. Ramsay, pp. 340 sqq.

value[1]. The Apology of Aristides[2] is on the same lines, and contains practically no new historical information.

The Apology of Aristides[3] is assigned to the year 125 A.D. by Eusebius, but was probably presented to Hadrian in 129 A.D., while that of Quadratus[4] belongs to the year 126 A.D. Before that time Hadrian had shown that he was inclined to go even further than Trajan in practical measures of mercy, though there seems no ground for believing with Hardy[5] that he abolished punishment for the "nomen." In order to understand the significance of Hadrian's rescript concerning the Christians we must first find out the circumstances under which it was written. Orosius[6] is wrong in saying that it was written in consequence of the Apologies of Quadratus and Aristides, for they were presented to Hadrian after 125 A.D., and we shall see that the date of the rescript is not later than 123 A.D.

The province of Asia was the real centre of the Christian religion at this time[7], but the habits of the Asiatics were strongly in opposition to Christian teaching, and popular feeling was here very bitter against the Christians. Moreover the province swarmed with persons[8] ready to become "delatores," and consequently, in spite of Trajan's wish for mild treatment, Christian prosecutions must have been frequent. In consequence

---

[1] Cf. Quadratus ap. Euseb. *H. E.* iv. 3.
[2] *Apol. of Aristides* (Texts and Studies).
[3] Euseb. *Chron.* ad ann.; Ramsay, p. 341.
[4] J. R. Harris puts both about 140 A.D., but his arguments are not conclusive. (Texts and Studies, Vol. i. No. 1, pp. 6—19.)
[5] Hardy, p. 143.   [6] Oros. 7, 13.
[7] Hardy, p. 142.   [8] Momms. *Röm. Gesch.* v. 333 sqq.

of the exceptional state of affairs in the province the governor, Serennius Granianus, had made a report to Hadrian, and Hadrian's rescript followed in the next year to the new governor, Minucius Fundanus. Now Granianus was consul in 106 A.D., Fundanus in 107 A.D.[1], and they would therefore reach the proconsulship of Asia not later than 121—2 A.D. and 122—3 A.D. respectively[2]. Accordingly we may conclude that Hadrian's rescript to Fundanus is not later than 123 A.D. Eusebius[3] commenting on it says that Hadrian wrote to Minucius Fundanus, *procos. Asiae*, ordering that no one should be put to death as a Christian without a definite charge and reasonable accusation. The text of the rescript, as preserved in Justin Martyr's first Apology, is as follows[4]:—

"Hadrianus Minucio Fundano. Accepi litteras ad me scriptas a decessore tuo Serennio Graniano clarissimo viro; et non placet mihi relationem silentio praeterire, ne et innoxii perturbentur et calumniatoribus latrocinandi tribuatur occasio. Itaque si evidenter provinciales huic petitioni suae adesse volent adversum Christianos, ut pro tribunali eos in aliquo arguant, hoc eis exequi non prohibeo; precibus autem in hoc solis et adclamationibus uti, eis non permitto. Etenim multo aequius est, si quis volet accusare, te cognoscere de obiectis: si quis igitur accuset et probet adversum leges quicquam agere memoratos homines, pro merito peccatorum etiam supplicia statues. Illud mehercle magnopere curabis, ut si quis calumniae gratia quemquam horum postulaverit reum, in hunc pro sua nequitia suppliciis saevioribus vindices."

This was indeed an attempt to wink at Christianity and to discourage persecution as far as possible, but it

---

[1] Klein, *Fast. cons.* p. 56. [2] Cf. Waddington, *Fast. Asiat.* p. 12.
[3] Euseb. *H. E.* iv. 8. [4] Just. Mart. *Apol.* 1, 68.

was no surrender of the principle that the "nomen ipsum" was illegal. In the first place provincials were distinctly allowed to appear in court and to try to get a conviction against Christians, while a few lines further on Hadrian orders the governor to punish the Christians, "si quis...accuset et probet *adversum leges* quicquam agere memoratos homines." But he does not state definitely the nature of the conviction, nor the laws which Christians might be proved to be breaking; and this vagueness is probably intentional. From a strictly legal point of view Hadrian saw that the "nomen ipsum" was a crime and that it could be brought under the head of *Maiestas*—a refusal to join in the state-worship. Practically however he desired to hint to the provincial governors that his personal view was in favour of punishment for the "flagitia cohaerentia nomini" only. He could not break through the traditional policy, but he made a determined effort to throw his personal influence in favour of complete toleration. He forbade the use of mere cries and denunciations; he required definite proof of Christianity; he decided that the prosecutor must come forward openly to support his charge and thereby incur the ill-will of a large section of provincials; he threatened heavy penalties against those who made vexatious indictments[1], e.g. to extort money. But if in spite of all this a prosecutor came forward and proved his charge of Christianity, not even the Emperor himself was strong enough to alter the course of the law.

The conduct of Hadrian in this matter was such

---

[1] Cf. Tert. *ad Scap.* 4.

as might have been expected from all that is known of the religious side of his character. Tertullian[1] says that he was "curiositatum omnium explorator," and Lampridius in his life of Alexander Severus[2] states that Hadrian intended to build a temple to Christ, and indeed did build in many places temples without statues for the purpose of setting up the Christian religion, and would have established that religion if he had not been dissuaded by his advisers. But, though unable actively to patronize Christianity, Hadrian must undoubtedly have freed the Christians from persecution to a great extent. Indeed the position of an informer against Christians was an unenviable one[3]. He stood in danger of being held responsible for any popular outbreak which might follow the information; he had no hope of reward; and lastly the Christians were becoming a large body, whose ill-will might be unpleasant. Prosecution would then generally come only from a strong corporation of those[4] whose trade had been injured, or from persons instigated by a strong feeling of revenge[5].

We are now in a position to estimate with a certain degree of confidence the relation in which the Christians stood to the Imperial government of Rome at the commencement of the reign of Antoninus Pius. It will be necessary to include in this estimate the general tendencies manifested by Trajan and Hadrian towards merciful treatment so long as order was preserved; but care must be taken to exclude the per-

[1] Tert. *Apol.* 5; cf. Dio C. lxix. 5 and 11.
[2] v. *Alex. Sev.* 43, 6 and 7.
[3] Cf. Ramsay, pp. 324—5.
[4] Cf. Pliny-Traj. *Ep.* 96, 10.
[5] Cf. Just. Mart. *Apol.* 2, 2.

sonal bias which Hadrian himself seems to have had in favour of Christianity. For while the general tendencies of Imperial government might bind a succeeding Emperor, the personal feelings of one Emperor would end with his death.

1. In the first place it had become customary for the Imperial government to check persecution as far as possible[1]. A conclusion had been arrived at that politically there was no danger to be expected from the Christians. The incompatibility of Christianity with state-worship was in reality a religious and not a political matter, and Pliny[2] had shown it to be such, when he could find nothing more alarming in Christianity than a "superstitio prava immodica." Again, on grounds of morality Christianity was void of offence. Pliny had shown that, in the cases at least which had come before him in Bithynia-Pontus, the Christians were leading a harmless and moral life, that they bound themselves to abstain from all manner of crimes and that their meetings were orderly and not the scenes of licence and debauchery. On social and economic grounds objection might still be taken to the Christians; they would not join in the ordinary life and amusements of the Roman people and their religion might cause disturbances in trade, as it did in Pliny's province. If then Christianity caused any strong feeling, it was open for individuals to prosecute the Christians in a court of law[3]. But anonymous charges were strictly forbidden, as was anything in the nature of a purely vexatious prosecution. Proof

[1] Euseb. *H. E.* iii. 33; Just. M. *Apol.* 1, 68.
[2] Pliny-Traj. *Ep.* 96.   [3] Cf. Hadrian's rescript.

had to be obtained that the accused was a Christian, and mere abuse and denunciation were to be disregarded.. The Imperial government in fact, while admitting the illegality of Christianity, considered that the Christians were not worth persecuting; persecution was a greater source of danger to the public peace than was Christianity itself. The Emperors held to the belief "Deorum iniuriae dis curae[1]," and it was therefore their aim to preserve order rather than to defend religion[2]. Accordingly they discouraged persecution.

2. We have next to remark that there was as a rule no official effort to seek out Christians. This might seem an inevitable deduction from the fact that the Emperors themselves discouraged persecution, but that is hardly the case. The Emperors objected to persecution, but at the same time admitted the illegality of Christianity; and this dual aspect of the case allowed to provincial governors a freer hand in their dealings with Christianity than they had in other matters. Trajan had written to Pliny "conquirendi non sunt[3]," and the tenor of Hadrian's rescript to Fundanus[4] had been even more merciful than that of Trajan's letter, imposing certain restrictions even on private prosecutors. Accordingly private prosecution was the usual course, as may be seen from the account of the Acta Martyrum Scilitanorum and the martyrdom of Ptolemaeus[5] in Rome, while further proof is found in the comparatively small number of Christians

[1] Ramsay, p. 206.
[2] Hardy, p. 140.
[3] Pliny-Traj. *Ep.* 97.
[4] Just. M. *Apol.* 1, 68.
[5] Just. M. *Apol.* 2, 2.

who had been put to death up to Origen's time[1]. But much depended on the actual condition of each province and the character of the provincial governor[2]. For while Pudens, who was governor of Crete before 166 A.D.[3], might tear up an indictment of Christians, because the accuser's name was not upon it and because he suspected an attempt to blackmail[4], other provincial magistrates, such as the Roman representative at Lugdunum in 177 A.D., might even go so far as to give way to the mob and to instigate a search for Christians[5].

3. The government did not as a rule seek out Christians, and a private person prosecuting on his own responsibility might find the ill-will of a large body like the Christians a source of no little danger[6]. Christians were accordingly left for the most part undisturbed, until some special circumstance occasioned an outbreak of strong popular feeling. It is not necessary to do more than briefly mention again the causes of this popular hatred:—(a) Christian "atheism" or refusal to worship recognized deities. (b) Contempt of Christians for social habits and amusements, and their interference with trade. (c) Popular belief in the moral guilt of Christians. (d) Their assumed re-

---

[1] Orig. c. Cels. iii. 8.

[2] An instance of the variations due to the varying character of governors is found in the fact that merciful governors, when testing for Christianity, allowed the prisoners to swear "per salutem Caesaris," an allowable oath, instead of "per genium Caesaris," which was a form not allowed by Christians. Dig. 48, 17, 1 and 2; Tert. Apol. 32.

[3] C. I. L. viii. 5354.   [4] Tert. ad Scap. 4.

[5] Euseb. H. E. v. 1, 14; Orig. c. Cels. viii. 69.

[6] Ramsay, pp. 324—6.

sponsibility for all calamities, which might occur. Eusebius, Tertullian and Justin Martyr[1] all bear witness to the fact that the persecutions of Christians were for the most part due to the attacks of the mob— ἐξ ἐπιθέσεως τῶν κατὰ πόλεις δήμων—led as in the case of Justin's martyrdom by such men as Crescens. In these cases the provincial governors[2] were sometimes either unable or unwilling to suppress the disorders and became mere instruments in the hands of the mob. Such was the case in the outbreak at Smyrna, which culminated in the martyrdom of Polycarp[3], and it would seem that similar riots were common in many Greek cities. Antoninus at least found it necessary to address a letter[4] to various Greek cities strictly forbidding such disorders, while the rescript of Hadrian to Minucius Fundanus[5] points to the same state of affairs in Asia. Popular hatred was thus the chief source of danger to the Christians.

4. Trajan had laid it down as a strict rule[6] that if a Christian recanted he should be immediately pardoned, and Justin Martyr notes—with a protest against the fact—that this policy was still continued in the reign of Antoninus Pius[7]. It was in fact a permanent policy, and the exception to it at Lugdunum in 177 A.D. was due in part to charges of immorality

---

[1] Euseb. *H. E.* v. 5; Tert. *Apol.* 35, 37, 49, 50; Just. M. *Apol.* 2, 3.
[2] Euseb. *H. E.* iii. 33.
[3] Euseb. *H. E.* iv. 15, 6; cf. Ruinart, *Acta Polyc.* p. 31.
[4] Euseb. *H. E.* iv. 26, 10.
[5] Just. M. *Apol.* 1, 68; Euseb. *H. E.* iv. 9.
[6] Pliny-Traj. *Ep.* 97.
[7] Just. M. *Apol.* 1. 4; cf. Orig. *c. Cels.* ii. 13.

brought against the Christians, and was even then disapproved of by the Emperor[1]. Torture, which was frequently applied to secure recantation, was originally introduced into these trials for the purpose of breaking down the "obstinatio" of the Christians, and as a rough means of saving them from the consequences of their own steadfastness[2]. But there is no need of evidence to show that torture was at times diverted from its original use and abused in a most flagrant manner.

5. We have estimated the practical position of the Christians in their relations with Rome; we now come to the legal basis of their position, a basis, which had remained exactly the same from the time of Nero to the time of Antoninus Pius in spite of the variations in practice between one reign and another. That legal basis, which had remained unchanged for some eighty years, may be expressed in the words:—Christianity "per se," i.e. the "nomen ipsum," is contrary to law[3]. It is a point which cannot be insisted on too strongly. Even Hardy[4] seems to forget it at times. He says that, when Christianity came under the head of *Maiestas*, (—if indeed it were ever tried under any other head[5]—) "more definite proof was required." Proof of what? The accused was required to perform acts of worship to the Emperor's image. If he were a resolute Christian, he refused and no further proof was wanted, i.e. the

[1] Euseb. *H. E.* v. 1, 33 and 47.
[2] Tert. *ad Scap.* 4; Just. *Dial. c. Tryph.* 110.
[3] Just. M. *Apol.* 1. 4, 11, 45; 2. 2; Tert. *Apol.* 2; Hermas, *Simil.* 9, 28; Athenagoras ii. 3.
[4] Hardy, p. 144.   [5] Momms. *Hist. Zeitsch.* lxiv. p. 396.

mere fact of his Christianity, quite apart from any considerations of character or crime, constituted an insult to the Emperor's majesty and insured a conviction under the head of *Maiestas*.

There is one point more which must be dealt with before passing on to consider the special relations of Antoninus Pius to the Christians, and that is the value of the evidence of Apologists[1]. They were writing for Imperial readers, for the very men who would be most likely to know the truth or falsehood of the Apologists' statements. It is therefore practically certain that the Apologists set down no material falsehoods in their writings. But at the same time they had no objection to improving their case by a suppression of the truth. For instance, it was to their advantage to make the immediately preceding times appear more favourable than they really were in order to give the Emperor a precedent for an increase of mercy. Accordingly we find Justin[2] citing the favourable rescript of Hadrian to Fundanus, but omitting all mention of the murder of Telesphorus; while Melito cites letters of Antoninus Pius forbidding disorderly attacks on the Christians, but ignores Polycarp's martyrdom[3]. It must then be remembered that, while there is no reason to doubt the facts actually mentioned by Apologists, there is also no reason to regard them as trustworthy historians.

It is not necessary in a treatise of this nature to refer at length to the inner organization of the Christians[4] which existed at the time of Antoninus Pius,

---

[1] Hardy, pp. 131, 132; Ramsay, pp. 341 sqq.
[2] Just. M. *Apol.* 1, 68. [3] Melito, ap. Euseb. *H. E.* iv. 26, 10.
[4] Wiltsch, *Geog. and Statist. of the Church.*

but a few words with regard to the extent of Christianity and the mutual relations of Christian communities at this period may be desirable. Wiltsch gives a long list of the bishops holding office in Asia Minor during the early days of Christianity [1], from which it is manifest that the greater part of the district must have been perfectly familiar with Christianity and have had a well-developed Christian organization existing in it. Pliny's letter to Trajan [2] may be taken as ample confirmation for this view, while from Eusebius it is plain that the Christian communities maintained close relations with one another and informed one another of all news affecting the Christians. The report of Ignatius's impending martyrdom was rapidly spread through Asia [3], so that deputations from various centres came to meet him on his way, while the Christians of Smyrna sent abroad the news of Polycarp's death [4].

Further east, Christianity spread to Edessa, and it is supposed that Prince Abgarus of Edessa was himself a Christian [5]. Syria and Palestine were of course centres of Christianity, and Antioch was regarded as the third town in importance in the Christian world [6]. In the south also Christianity was firmly established, and Alexandria was second only to Rome in its Christian importance. Throughout Spain [7] there were Christians by the close of the second century A.D., while in Gaul they were prominent enough to excite a violent persecution

---

[1] Wiltsch, i. pp. 47—49.
[2] Pliny-Traj. *Ep.* 96.
[3] Euseb. *H. E.* iii. 36.
[4] Euseb. *H. E.* iv. 15.
[5] Cf. "vir sanctus" *Chron. Edess.* viii.
[6] Anacletus, *Ep.* iii. 3.
[7] Cf. Tert. *adv. Iudaeos.*

at Lugdunum in 177 A.D.[1] Greece was also well acquainted with Christianity, and it is interesting to note that the first bishop of Heraclea in Thrace was a contemporary of Antoninus Pius[2]. In Italy itself there were numerous bishops by 175 A.D.[3]

As to the organization of the Church, Rome was regarded as its governing head, Alexandria as the second city, and Antioch as the third[4]; the Roman bishops exercised authority over and even punished smaller dignitaries not in Italy alone but also in Gaul[5]. Anacletus, who became bishop of Rome in 104 A.D., speaks of four orders in the Church[6]:—1. The Roman pontiff. 2. The Patriarchs or heads of the Church in provincial capitals. 3. The Metropolitans or bishops of other large towns. 4. Ordinary bishops. Anicetus, bishop of Rome from 157 A.D., confirms this account[7].

There was a definite organization of the Church in the reign of Antoninus Pius, but it was so obviously free from all political designs that the Roman Emperors —though they cannot have been ignorant of its existence—allowed it to remain unmolested. Attacks that were made upon Christianity were directed not against Christian organization, but against individual Christians. This was in itself a sign that the government was convinced of the harmlessness of Christianity and was willing in practice to tolerate it, until popular feeling demanded the expression in action of the

---

[1] Euseb. *H. E.* v. 1.
[2] Le Quien, ii. 27 sq.
[3] Soter, *Ep.* i. and ii.
[4] Anacletus, *Ep.* iii. § 3.
[5] Anicetus, *Ep. ad Gall. Episc.* § 3.
[6] Anacletus, *Ep.* ii. § 4.
[7] Anicetus, *Ep. ad Gall. Episc.* § 2; Zonaras, xii. P. 1, 594 A.

unaltered but tacitly ignored principle that Christianity was illegal.

Antoninus Pius was strongly attached to the older or mythological varieties of Roman worship, and was making an endeavour to restore to this side of the state religion some of the vitality which it had had under the Republic[1]. This would of course place him strongly in opposition to Christianity, but at the same time would divert his attention to some extent from the worship of Emperors—which was the ordinary stumbling-block of the Christians. He undoubtedly kept up the Imperial worship[2], but the Christians might be thankful for the fact that Antoninus Pius's religious bent was chiefly towards a different side of religion. Again, the Emperor was of a merciful and orderly character. He would therefore be unwilling to seek out Christians or to permit his officials to do so. Still more would he be opposed to riotous popular demonstrations against the obnoxious religion. On the whole then it is clear that the general tendency of Pius's government would be to follow out the policy of Trajan and Hadrian— a policy of non-interference—until private persons had made a definite charge against Christians. But it is probable that, when this charge had been made, he was led by his devotion to religion to be more strict than Hadrian in requiring the punishment of those who would not recant.

In the first year of Antoninus Pius's reign Telesphorus[3], who had held the bishopric of Rome for nearly

[1] Cf. G. Boissier, *La Religion Romaine*, 1, 360—361 and 2, 192.
[2] Cf. G. Boissier, *La Religion Romaine*, 1, 197—202.
[3] Zonaras, xii. P. 1, 594 A; Irenaeus, ap. Euseb. *H. E.* iv. 10.

eleven years, was martyred; but we have no record of the circumstances under which his death took place. In the absence of any mention of other martyrdoms at the same time, it is a probable supposition that Telesphorus was denounced by private enemies and put to death in the ordinary course as guilty under the "leges maiestatis." He was succeeded by Hyginus[1], who held office from 138 A.D. to 142 A.D. In the time of Hyginus the Christians seem to have been unmolested, for no instance of persecution can be dated with any certainty within these four years. Irenaeus however—quoted by Eusebius and referred to by Zonaras—says that during this period the Christian religion suffered considerably from heresies introduced by Valentinus, Cerdo and Marcion. It is not within the scope of this treatise to investigate the nature of these heresies. But the fact that the Christian body had time to be divided and subjected to bitter internal disputes is some confirmation for the view that Christianity was not at that moment suffering from the oppressive, but at the same time uniting, burden of persecution. Hyginus was succeeded in the year 142 A.D. by a bishop named Pius[2], while about the same time Marcus became bishop of Alexandria, holding the office till he was succeeded ten years later by Celadion.

During the Episcopate of Pius there was a typical case of persecution for revenge in Rome. Q. Lollius Urbicus was *praefectus urbi* under Antoninus Pius, the most probable period for his tenure of this office

---

[1] Zon. *l. c.*; Euseb. *l. c.*
[2] Euseb. *H. E.* iv. 12; Zonaras *l.c.*

being about 152 A.D.[1], and during his prefecture the case occurred[2]. There lived at Rome a married couple of bad character, but at length the woman was converted to Christianity and used her utmost endeavours to convert her husband also. But her conversion only irritated him, and finally in disgust at his general conduct she applied for and obtained a divorce. Incensed at this her husband attacked Ptolemaeus, who had been the instrument of her conversion. By means of an accommodating centurion the husband managed to get Ptolemaeus thrown into prison and then denounced him as a Christian. Ptolemaeus was detained in prison for some time and at length came before Q. Lollius Urbicus. The test for Christianity was put to him, he acknowledged his religion and refused to worship the Emperor's image; Urbicus thereupon condemned him to death. But a certain Lucius, who was present in the court, called out that Ptolemaeus had done no harm and that Urbicus was not acting worthily of an εὐσεβὴς Emperor, of a φιλοσόφου Καίσαρος υἱὸς, or of the sacred Senate; and he avowed that he himself was a Christian also. Lucius was thereupon condemned in the same way as Ptolemaeus and the incident was ended.

One or two points at least are clear from this narrative; on the one hand that the initiative rested with private accusers and that a clear case of Christianity had to be made out; on the other that the "nomen ipsum" was punishable, and that to clear up all doubts as to a prisoner's Christianity tests were ad-

---

[1] Borghesi, Œuvres, ix. 295.
[2] Just. Mart. Apol. 2, 2; Euseb. H. E. iv. 17.

ministered to him in court. It may also fairly be supposed from the action of this Lucius that an opinion had spread abroad that the Emperors themselves were unwilling to punish for the "nomen,"— an opinion to which Hadrian's actions might have lent some support, though in reality Hadrian did not alter the law on the subject. Further we may remark that the management of Christians was now as formerly a police affair[1]. Q. Lollius Urbicus in virtue of the executive powers vested in him as chief police magistrate of the city[2] sentenced Ptolemaeus and Lucius, while in the provinces the provincial governors would have exercised similar powers[3].

A few years after these cases of persecution in Rome a persecution of a more general nature broke out in Smyrna, which ended in the martyrdom of Polycarp. It is a difficult matter to determine with any certainty the date of this outbreak, and Eusebius[4] apparently groups it with incidents which happened in the reign of M. Aurelius; but he does not state distinctly that the outbreak was in Marcus's reign. Waddington[5] after carefully considering the question gives the year 155 A.D. as the most probable date of Polycarp's martyrdom, and, though his arguments are not entirely conclusive, they have a considerable amount of evidence to support them. Eusebius places Polycarp's martyrdom in the year of the proconsulship of Statius Quadratus on the 7th of the Calends of May

---

[1] Momms., *Hist. Zeitsch.* lxiv. p. 398.   [2] Cf. Tac. *Ann.* vi. 11.
[3] *Dig.* 1, 18, 13.   [4] Euseb. *H. E.* iv. 15. § 1.
[5] Wadd., *Mém. sur la vie du Rhéteur Aristide* (*Mém. de l'Acad.* 1867), pp. 214—235.

(Lat. Version—7th of the Calends of *March*) on a Sabbath. Now Waddington shows that Severus was proconsul in 153-154 A.D., and on the testimony of Aristides says that Quadratus was proconsul the year after, *i.e.* in 154-155 A.D.[1] This corresponds with the fact that a L. Statius Quadratus was consul in 141 A.D., since 12—15 years was the interval of time, which at this period elapsed between a consulship and a pro-consulship[2]. At the same time the 7th of the Calends of March (Feb. 23) was a Sabbath in 155 A.D. —the 7th of the Calends of May being apparently an error in writing. We need therefore only assume that Eusebius has made an error of arrangement in placing Polycarp's martyrdom among the events of M. Aurelius's reign, and if that assumption be made we may accept Waddington's date of 155 A.D.[3] In support of this assumption attention should be drawn to a similar confusion between Antoninus Pius and M. Aurelius, which Waddington omits to mention. In the case of the rescript of Antoninus Pius[4] to τὸ κοινὸν τῆς 'Ασίας, Eusebius states that it was written by ὁ αὐτὸς βασιλεύς, using this phrase where it can only refer to Antoninus Pius[5]; but immediately afterwards he begins the text of the rescript, giving as the name of its author M. Aurelius. Probably Eusebius's confused statement is due to the fact that he did not

[1] Arist. (Dind.), 1. 523: *C. I. G.* 3410.
[2] Wadd., pp. 240, 241.
[3] Cf. for the date, Lightfoot, *Apostolic Fathers*, II. 1. pp. 629—695.
[4] Euseb. *H. E.* iv. 13.
[5] The question as to whether the rescript is genuine does not affect the importance of Eusebius's confusion.

distinguish between the commencement of Marcus's nominal Empire (147 A.D.) and the commencement of his real power (161 A.D.). The date at the head of the rescript is:—M. Aurelius Tr. P. xv. Cos. iii,—which should in all probability be read—Antoninus Pius Tr. P. xv. Cos. iii,—since Eusebius has just before ascribed the rescript to Antoninus Pius; the error is not unnatural, since the power of M. Aurelius after 147 A.D. was not altogether nominal. If this view of the case be adopted, the date of the rescript will be 152 A.D., which accords well with the reference contained in its text to the earthquake of 151—152 A.D. in Asia Minor[1].

What was the occasion of the rescript we do not know. Its reference to the recent earthquake makes it probable that the heathen populace had ascribed in their usual fashion the responsibility for that disaster to the Christians and had in consequence made disorderly attacks on them[2], which called for a rebuke and admonition from the Emperor. There is nothing in the rescript with the exception of the last clause, which need cause any doubt as to its genuine character or any question as to whether Antoninus Pius was departing from the traditional Imperial policy. If it be genuine, the Emperor[3] commences with a statement of the principle "Deorum iniuriae dis curae," which is a way of saying that Christians are not punished on religious grounds, but because they will not perform a duty required by the State, *i.e.* the duty of worshipping the Emperors. He then discourages disorderly persecutions[4] for two reasons—that the

[1] Euseb. *H. E.* iv. 13. § 4. [2] Tert. *Apol.* 40.
[3] Euseb. *H. E.* iv. 13. § 2. [4] *Ibid.*, §§ 3—5.

Christians on the one hand were benefited by persecution, and that their persecutors on the other had plenty of faults of their own to correct. Next he affirms[1] his intention of adhering to Hadrian's plan of leaving Christians alone, if they keep free from all suspicion of political designs. By this Antoninus Pius does not imply that he had any reason to fear a conspiracy among the Christians; he only means that he will regard the Christian refusal to worship Emperors, when challenged to do so in a court of law, as a breach of the "leges maiestatis," *i.e.* as high treason, a political offence[2]. Finally in the last clause[3] the Emperor is made to say that if any one accuses a Christian ὡς δὴ τοιοῦτον, the accused shall be liberated in spite of his Christianity, while the accuser shall himself be liable to prosecution. If this clause is to be regarded as genuine, the only possible conclusion is that Antoninus Pius entirely reversed the policy of previous Emperors and forbade prosecution for the "nomen." But this view does not harmonize with the preceding statement in the rescript that the policy of the previous Emperors was to be maintained. It is probable that this last sentence is of later date than the rest of the rescript. The Christians in after years[4] regarded the reign of Antoninus Pius as an exceptionally favourable period, and they accounted for the favour shown to them not by the personal character of the Emperor but by a supposed change in the law. Accordingly

---

[1] Euseb. *H. E.* iv. 13. § 6.
[2] Cf. G. Boissier, *La Religion Romaine*, i. pp. 79 and 105.
[3] Euseb. *H. E.* iv. 13. § 7.
[4] Sulp. Sev. *Chron.* 2. 32; Oros. 7. 14, etc.

some Christian writer tacked on to the rescript a remark which he wrongly considered appropriate. Another alternative is to deny the genuine character of the whole rescript, but this seems too decided a course in view of the accuracy and trustworthiness of all its clauses but the last. Even if it be not genuine, the larger part of the rescript is strictly in accord with what is known of Antoninus Pius's policy from other sources. Other letters[1], which he wrote to the authorities at Larissa, Thessalonica, Athens[2] and to all the Greeks, must have been similar in purport to the first part of this rescript.

But the letters which were sent to various cities do not seem to have had the desired effect, and matters came to a crisis in Smyrna probably in 155 A.D.[3] There had been some minor persecutions in this city, either at the close of 154 A.D. or the commencement of 155 A.D., but the populace soon began to tire of the ordinary routine of trial and condemnation and clamoured for some special excitement. Polycarp was at this time bishop of Smyrna, an old man and one who had known Ignatius well[4]. He had not the fiery and uncompromising nature of Ignatius, but rather endeavoured to keep peace with all men. In face of the disturbances in Smyrna, his friends entreated Polycarp to hide himself,

---

[1] Melito, ap. Euseb. *H. E.* iv. 26. One at least of these letters was probably written after Polycarp's death.

[2] Cf. Martyrdom of Publius, Bishop of Athens, about this time. Euseb. *H. E.* iv. 23.

[3] Euseb. *H. E.* iv. 15. (Letter from Church of Smyrna describing the events.)

[4] Polyc. *ad Philipp.* 9. 13.

and the aged bishop at length consented to retire into the country districts. But, taking no special precautions, he was arrested and brought back into the city on a Sabbath—Feb. 23rd, 155 A.D. Being led before the proconsul, he repeated willingly enough after the magistrate the words αἶρε τοὺς ἀθέους, but he refused to swear by Καίσαρος τύχη or to blaspheme Christ. The proconsul, Statius Quadratus, evidently wished to spare Polycarp, or he would not have challenged him to swear by Καίσαρος τύχη, i.e. *per salutem Caesaris*—a less objectionable form of oath to Christians than *per genium Caesaris*[1]; but he was in the hands of the mob, and when Polycarp endeavoured to reason with him, ἔφη ὁ ἀνθύπατος 'πεῖσαι τὸν δῆμον.' Polycarp, however, refused to recognize the mob as his judges. He acknowledged his Christianity and refused to yield to threats. Polycarp had now refused to comply with the two tests; he would not worship the Emperor, even to the limited extent that was involved in swearing *per salutem Caesaris*, and he would not deny his Christianity. There was therefore no escape for him. The proconsul indeed went so far as to make a last appeal to the mob[2],—though his appeal seems rather like a mere attempt to shift the responsibility on to the shoulders of the mob. But the mob insisted that Polycarp should suffer death, and that too by the unusual method of burning. Quadratus gave way, and Polycarp was burnt to death. In this case besides yielding weakly to the mob, both generally and in the choice of the means of execution, Quadratus permitted

[1] *Dig.* 48, 17, 1 and 2; Tert. *Apol.* 32.
[2] Euseb. *H. E.* iv. 15. § 25.

a definite illegality. It does not appear that a precise charge was made against Polycarp in the name of any individual accuser. He was merely set upon by the mob, and therefore the proconsul ought not to have taken any account of the charge at all, but should have refused to try the case and have liberated Polycarp.

It is not probable that Antoninus Pius passed over this violation of law and order without some severe comment, and there were at the same time riots against Christians in Pergamos, which called for a similar rebuke[1]. Melito states that Antoninus Pius wrote among other letters concerning Christians one to "all the Greeks," forbidding any riotous attacks upon the objectionable sect[2]. It has been assumed with great probability that this letter was written to the Greeks of Asia Minor in consequence of the riots in Smyrna and Pergamos[3].

To return now to the Christians in Rome, we find that Pius, after holding the bishopric for 15 years, died in 157 A.D.[4] and was succeeded by Anicetus. The great figure in the Christian world at this time was Justin Martyr, who had originally been a pagan philosopher, and was in consequence able to take a broader view of the aims of Christianity than many of his contemporaries. He now worked energetically to consolidate the Christian body internally and to save it from external persecution ἐν φιλοσόφου σχήματι πρεσβεύων τὸν θεῖον λόγον καὶ τοῖς ὑπὲρ τῆς πίστεως ἐναγωνιζόμενος συγγράμμασιν. The Episcopate of

---

[1] Euseb. *H. E.* iv. 15. § 48.   [2] Euseb. *H. E.* iv. 26.
[3] Ramsay, p. 331.
[4] Zonaras, xii. P. 1. 594 B; Euseb. *H. E.* iv. 13.

Anicetus lasted until after the death of Antoninus Pius, and the absence of information for the years 157—161 A.D. goes to show that for the Christians as well as for the other members of the Roman Empire the closing years of Antoninus's reign were years of peace.

To those writers like Sulpicius Severus or Orosius[1], who chronicled the history of the Christians in the barest outline, the reign of Antoninus Pius seemed a time of peace and the Emperor a protector of the Christians; while Eusebius[2] himself says that Antoninus was much influenced in favour of the Christians by Justin Martyr. But it has been shown that a considerable amount of persecution did take place under this Emperor[3]. Indeed, owing to the fact that contemporary Christian accounts were just beginning to be written, more than the usual amount of evidence bearing on persecution remains. And the rescript to τὸ κοινὸν τῆς 'Ασίας so far from being exceptionally favourable is a distinct declaration—in all its clauses save the last—of adherence to traditional policy. The mistaken idea arose partly from an erroneous belief that Antoninus Pius's merciful character must have found expression in exceptional mercy towards Christians, partly from the inability of Christian writers to distinguish between the legal and the practical position of Christians. Like his predecessors, Antoninus Pius felt himself bound to punish Christians as such, when they were properly accused and properly convicted. But like his predecessors he was unwilling to interfere with

---

[1] Sulp. Sev. *Chron.* 2. 32; Oros. 7. 14.
[2] Euseb. *H. E.* iv. 12.
[3] Cf. Lightfoot, *Apost. Fathers* II. 1. p. 493.

Christianity unless forced to do so, and still more unwilling to tolerate anything in the nature of a disorderly riot against the Christians.

Before passing on from the general position of Christianity in this reign, reference may be made to the intense hostility of the Jews to the Christians at this period. Hadrian had forbidden Jews to reside in Jerusalem[1] or Aelia, as it was now called, while the Christians, who were not excluded, established a community with a bishop in that city[2]. Thus the Jews had a strong reason for envying the Christians, and when Antoninus Pius went on to repress Judaism still further, and forbade Gentiles under pain of death to take part in Jewish worship[3], the feeling of jealousy was still further increased. Tertullian[4], speaking on the subject, was justified in saying,—"Tot hostes eius (*i.e.* of Christianity) quot extranei et quidem proprie ex aemulatione Iudaei."

It now remains to estimate the feelings of the educated classes towards Christianity—feelings, which will be found to be those of contempt and assumed ignorance. But the expression of contempt is somewhat overdone, and the laboured sarcasm of Lucian[5] is an evidence that educated Rome was beginning to feel slightly uneasy in the presence of this new and unintelligible movement. In his account of the supposed death of a certain Peregrinus Proteus, a piece of elaborate satire, which has already been described at length, Lucian paints a black sheep of Christianity

---

[1] Euseb. *H. E.* iv. 6. § 4. [2] Cf. Syncell. pp. 660, 661.
[3] *Dig.* 48, 8, 11. [4] Tert. *Apol.* 7.
[5] Lucian, περὶ τῆς Περεγρίνου τελευτῆς.

as a representative of the whole sect. His picture is near enough the truth to be a good satire on some of the failings of individual Christians, but it is an undoubted misrepresentation of the Christians as a whole and in all probability a wilful misrepresentation. It is a decided attempt to confuse the "flagitia cohaerentia nomini" with the "nomen ipsum." Pliny had seen that the "nomen" might be, and in fact generally was free from "flagitia." Other provincial governors, who came into contact with Christians, saw the same thing for themselves, while the traditional policy of the Emperors was an expression of this same belief in the harmlessness of Christianity. It is then extremely improbable that Lucian seriously believed in the immorality of Christianity[1]. He paints a picture, which may have been fairly true in a few instances, and which would have been an absurdity without these instances. But his implied statement that the picture is universally true, is an intentional misrepresentation. If the question be raised, why Lucian should have so misrepresented the case, the answer must be—partly indeed that he wished to amuse, partly that he had strong personal or class feeling. He felt that Christianity was a rebuke to the loose and empty life of the upper classes of Roman society, a challenge to their philosophy, and he wished by his ridicule to prevent that rebuke from taking shape in action.

[1] It is true that even in the last 20 years false charges of immoral practices have been believed against religious sects *for a short time or among uneducated classes*, *e.g.* against the Salvation Army in England and the Jews in Russia. But this is different from a lasting belief by educated men and is itself the outcome of class-feeling.

Whether Apuleius[1] is satirizing Christianity in his account of the transformation of a man into an ass is not certain, but having regard to the well-known scrawl found in Rome—a boy worshipping a crucified figure, which has an ass's head—it is at least possible that he is doing so. Aristides affects to ignore Christianity, referring to the Christians only once in a passage, where he ridicules the Cynics and compares them "to those impious Palestinians, good like them at sowing discord in families[2]." Celsus, who by common consent is agreed to have written in the reign of Antoninus Pius, wrote a work entitled Ἀληθὴς λόγος, in which he raised objection to various points insisted on by the Christians. Information as to the scope of this work must be derived from the reply to it, which Origen wrote at a later date[3]. From this reply it seems that Celsus entered into a more systematic and rational opposition to Christianity than his contemporaries. Among other points, to which he made reference, he opposed the idea that the universe was made with a view to its enjoyment by man[4]—a contention of many Apologists and the basis of much of their argument—and also disputed the claim of the Jews to be regarded as a specially favoured people and of the Christians to regard their Founder as divine[5].

While on the one side there is this attempt to resist or to ignore a movement, whose force was already partially felt and feared, on the other side Justin

---

[1] Apuleius, *Metam*.
[2] Arist. (Dind.), ii. 402.
[3] Orig. c. *Celsum*.
[4] *Ibid*. iv. §§ 23, 74, 77.
[5] *Ibid*. i. § 26; iv. § 32.

Martyr was endeavouring to combat the erroneous ideas, which were held on Christianity, and to represent this religion in its true light. His first Apology gives its own date[1] as 150 A.D., though this may be only approximate. However Eusebius[2] says that the rescript to τὸ κοινὸν τῆς Ἀσίας was written as a result of the impression produced on Antoninus Pius by Justin's first Apology, and we have seen reason to assign this rescript to the year 152 A.D. It is therefore not unlikely that the date 150 A.D. for the first Apology is very nearly an exact date. It is addressed to the Emperor and his adopted sons[3], and it is therefore concerned to a large extent with that, which was always the legal aspect of persecution—persecution for the "nomen ipsum." Accordingly Justin gives an exposition of Christianity, showing that it has much in common with the principles of Philosophy[4] laid down by Plato and other writers, and that its doctrines are calculated to make men useful, peaceable and law-abiding citizens[5]. Further in face of the infinite varieties of heathen religions which are all tolerated it is illogical to persecute people whose only offence is their name, especially when the miracles claimed by heathen religions are stranger than those claimed by Christianity[6]. Justin also assured the Emperor that there was no thought of political designs in Christianity, and that Christians would honour the Emperor in everything save in the matter of paying him worship[7].

[1] Just. M. *Apol.* 1. 46.
[2] Euseb. *H. E.* iv. 12.
[3] *Apol.* 1. 1.
[4] *Apol.* 1. §§ 5, 8, 20, 46, 60 ff.
[5] *Ib.* §§ 12—16, 27—29, etc.
[6] *Ib.* §§ 3, 19, 22, 24, 25, 54, 62.
[7] *Ib.* §§ 11, 17.

But Justin also set himself to combat the false ideas prevalent among the masses with regard to Christianity. He showed that there was no absurdity in the religion[1], that the charge of Atheism was unfounded[2], and above all that the accusation of immorality was an idle accusation with no evidence to support it[3]. The complaint that Christians severed themselves from the ordinary amusements[4] was better supported, but the severance was due to the fact that Christians looked rather to a future life than to the present. Finally[5] Justin implored the Emperor not to judge of the religion by its black sheep, but to look at Christianity by itself and to judge it on its own merits.

The second Apology[6] is assigned to various dates, but in consideration of the reference made to the prefecture of Q. Lollius Urbicus[7] as of recent date, it seems likely that this Apology was written soon after 152 A.D. It is in effect a summary of the arguments of the first Apology, but it contains a special reference to the hostility of educated Romans to Christianity. Crescens, whose philosophy showed itself principally in noise and boasting—so much so that Justin calls him φιλό-ψοφος and φιλόκομπος instead of φιλόσοφος[8]—had been loud in his denunciations of the Christians, calling them ἄθεοι just as the common mob would do. Moreover he cared not at all whether his denunciations were true or false. "But what," says Justin, "can you

---

[1] *Apol.* 1. §§ 13, 14, 18, 19, 21, 22, 48—53.   [2] *Ib.* §§ 5, 6, 9, 10.
[3] *Ib.* §§ 14, 29, 56—60, 65, 66.   [4] *Ib.* § 18.   [5] *Ib.* §§ 7, 67.
[6] Cf. Prof. Hort on the date of the two Apologies (*Journ. of Class. and Sacr. Philol.* III. 1856, pp. 155—193).
[7] Just. M. *Apol.* 2. 2.   [8] *Apol.* 2. 3.

expect from a Cynic, to whom everything is ἀδιάφορον?" Justin adds that he has already convicted Crescens of falsehood in open argument, but that Crescens will soon have his revenge by procuring Justin's martyrdom.

By these two Apologies Justin explained to the Emperor and to educated men in general the true facts concerning the Christians. He showed the claims which Christianity had on the consideration of intelligent people, and the inoffensive nature of Christian life and doctrines. But the Apologies would not perhaps be heard of by many Romans, and, even if they were, it was not to be expected that much immediate result would follow. They did not at any rate alter the fact that Christianity was in itself theoretically illegal, and though Eusebius[1] says that Antoninus Pius was induced by Justin to send the rescript to τὸ κοινὸν τῆς Ἀσίας, persecution still assailed the Christians. The truth is that since Trajan's time at least government-persecution had ceased and the troubles of Christianity were due to the unreasoning prejudices of the mob. These prejudices would hardly be affected by a thousand Apologies and there remained only two ways by which Christianity might be finally saved from persecution—one, that the Emperor should recognize the legality of Christianity and forbid all persecution whether orderly or disorderly, the other that the Christians should by their lives and actions win over the populace to regard them with tolerant eyes. We have seen that the Emperor refused to adopt the former course; the latter was a course which would need centuries before it would be crowned with complete success.

[1] Euseb. *H. E.* iv. 12.

INDEX.

Abgarus, Prince of Edessa, 77, 188.

Ad commune Asiae, rescript, 67, 194—197.

Aemilian way repaired, 54.

Africa, brigandage in, 69; attempt to make a road through the *Saltus Aurasius*, 70; Numidia freed from brigands, 70; active operations of Roman legions, 70; T. Varius Clemens sent from Spain, 71; Tingitana quieted, 71; date of the operations, 72; character of the outbreak, 72, 73.

Agriculture assisted by charitable endowment schemes, 122.

Alani, revolt of, 78.

Alimentariae, 121—122.

Anicetus, bishop of Rome, 199, 200.

Antium, aqueduct of Antoninus Pius at, 116.

Antoninus Pius, birth of, 7; name, 7; Gallic extraction, 7; connection with S. Gaul, 8, 56; older members of family, 8; home at Lorium, 9, 90, 91; education, 9, 10; property, 10, 11; early life, 11, 12; first consulship, 12; marriage, 13; children, 14; *quattuorvir consularis*, 15; *procos. Asiae*, 16, 17; admitted to *consilium Hadriani*, 17; adopted by Hadrian, 17—21; his care for Hadrian, 22, 23; position at close of Hadrian's reign, 22—24; coins of Hadrian and Antoninus jointly, 23.

Emperor, 24; his treatment of Senate, 27, 28, 30, 103—108; *pontifex maximus*, 28; *Pius*, 24, 28, 29; honours to his family, 29; *ludi circenses*, 29, 50, 94; *pater patriae*, 30, 38; love of theatre etc., 30, 94; second consulship, 32; third consulship, 39; Imperator II, 44; never triumphed, 44; restores damage caused by first earthquake, 47; death of his wife, 48—50; fourth consulship, 56; first decennial vows, 61, 62; character of his reign, 64, 97; confused with M. Aurelius, 67; restores damage caused by second earthquake, 69; visits Egypt, 75, 76; visits Syria, 74—80; second decennial vows, 83, 88, 89; death, 90, 91; canonization, 91, 92.

Personal appearance, 93; tastes, 94; κυμινοπρίστης, 94; religious zeal, 94; *civilitas*, 95; character, 96, 97; his relations with M. Aurelius and L. Verus, 98—102; his use of *consilium principis*, 112—114; his relations with the Italians, 115—122; public works in Italy, 116, 117; *alimentariae*, 121—122; his relations with the provinces, 122—130; public works, etc. in the provinces, 127, 128; justice of his arbitration, 129; mythological worship encouraged, 141—147, 190; no special attachment to Imperial cult, 148, 149, 190; position of Christians under Antoninus Pius, 181—206.

Apollonius, 95.

Appian as historical authority, 3.

Apuleius as historical authority, 2; his life and writings, 133—135; probably attacks Christianity, 134, 135, 203.

Aristides, (Apologist), 176—178; value of evidence of Apologists, 187.

Aristides, Aelius (Rhetorician), as historical authority, 2; his exaggeration, 3; persuades M. Aurelius to restore damage caused by second earthquake, 69; academic style, 135, 136; compared to Demosthenes, 136.

Armenia, King appointed over, 51, 77.

Arrian as historical authority, 3.

Arvales, M. Aurelius Master of, 99, 146; prominence of the college in this reign, 145, 146; record of their proceedings, 146.

Asia, prosperity of, 125.

Athens, buildings of Antoninus Pius at, 127.

'Αθεότης, Christians charged with, 162—164.

Augustales, Seviri, 118, 119.

Augustalium, ordo, 118, 119.

Aurelius Antoninus, M., as historical authority, 2; family of, 13, 98; adopted by Antoninus Pius, 20, 98; left in charge of affairs at Rome, 24, 98; betrothed to Galeria Faustina, 32, 99; early honours, 39, 99; first consulship, 39, 99; early coins, 39, 99; second consulship, 56, 99; marriage, 53, 58, 59, 100; birth of daughter, 59, 100; *tribunicia potestas*, 58, 59, 100; *proconsulare imperium*, 59, 100; *ius quintae relationis*, 59, 60, 100; his position, 60, 100, 101; twin children, 65; restores damage caused by second earthquake, 68; visits Syria, 80, 81; strong position at close of Antoninus Pius's reign, 90, 91; preferred before Verus, 98; Master of the Arvales, 99; chosen sole successor by Antoninus Pius, 102; takes Verus as his colleague, 102.

His writings, 136—138; Eclectic and Stoic, 136, 137; good sentiments but small literary merit, 137, 138; instructed in rhetoric by Fronto, 138.

Aurum Coronarium, 34—36; coins relating to, 35, 36; only partially accepted, 37, 115, 126; offered

INDEX. 209

'by Parthia and Scythia, 37; not sent by Britain, 41.
Authorities, varied nature of, 1—6.

Barchochebas, Jewish rebel, 175.
Bithynia laid waste by earthquake, 68.
Border-kings, influence of Antoninus Pius with, 123.
Brigantes, 41, 43.
Britain, war in, 39; date and incidents of war, 39—41; the Brigantes, 41; a mere revolt, 42; suppressed by Q. Lollius Urbicus, 42, 43; Brigantes driven northwards, 43; wall built on the lines of Agricola's defences, 43, 44.

Caieta, harbour built by Antoninus Pius at, 116.
Capua, amphitheatre of, 38, 116.
Carni and Catuli admitted to *Latinitas*, 117.
Carthage, 129.
Catilius Severus, discontent of, 12, 13, 23, 30, 107.
Celsus, author of Ἀληθὴς λόγος, 203.
Celsus, conspiracy of, 107.
Cerdo, heresy of, 191.
Chaeronea, Antoninus Pius's generosity to, 127.
Christianity, indirectly aided by attacks of satirists like Lucian, 132, 133, 201, 202; probably satirized by Apuleius, 134, 135, 203; absence of any strong antagonistic religion, 149; legal position of Christianity unaltered from 60 A.D. to 160 A.D., 150; at first considered a variety of Judaism, 153, 154; spreads in Asia Minor, 154.

Apparent political danger to Rome, 154; interference with social conditions, 154, 155; interference with trade, 155; *odium humani generis*, 155, 156; crimes alleged against Christianity, 156; relations of Claudius with the Christians, 156; Gentile Christians in Rome, 156, 157; persecution for *nomen ipsum*, 158—160, 166, 171, 172, 174, 178, 186, 192; identification of Christianity with *odium humani generis*, 158, 159; *obstinatio*, 158, 169, 186; *flagitia cohaerentia nomini*, 158, 202; occasion of Neronian persecution, 160; theoretically a standing persecution, 160; regulated by police, 160, 161, 165, 193; persecution put in force or suspended according to circumstances, 161, 184; immunity under Vespasian and Titus, 161; Domitian revives persecution, 161—166; political bias of persecution under Domitian, 163, 164; ἀθεότης and *molitor rerum novarum*, 162—164; Christians prosecuted under head of *Maiestas*, 162—165, 180, 186, 187, 191; tests for Christianity, 165, 184, 192, 193, 198; jurisdiction in Christian trials, 166, 193.

Pliny in Bithynia-Pontus, 166-174; Hetairiai suppressed, 167; Pliny's procedure, 167, 168; his investigations into Christi-

B. 14

anity, 169, 170; suggestions for merciful treatment, 170—172; Trajan authorizes mercy without surrendering the principle, 174, 175; Hadrian and Antoninus Pius follow the same course, 175, 180, 190; causes of subsequent persecutions, 175, 183—185; no state-persecution under Hadrian, 176, 183; rise of Apologists, 176—178; value of their evidence, 187; Asia the centre of Christianity, 178; rescript to Minucius Fundanus, 178, 179; persecution discouraged, 180—182, 197, 199; Hadrian supposed to have inclined to Christianity, 181.

Position of Christians at commencement of Antoninus Pius's reign, 181—187; torture in Christian trials, 186; unaltered legal position, 186, 200; extent and organization, 187—189; individuals not organization attacked, 189; Christians profit by unimportance of Imperial cult, 190; prosecution by private individuals, 190, 192; martyrdom of Telesphorus, 190, 191; Hyginus, 191; heresies, 191; Pius, bishop of Rome, 191, 199; bishops of Alexandria, 191; martyrdoms in prefecture of Q. Lollius Urbicus, 191—193; Christian belief in the mercy of Antoninus Pius, 192, 193; martyrdom of Polycarp, 193—199; rescript *ad commune Asiae*, 194—197; letters of Antoninus Pius forbidding persecution, 197, 199; Anicetus, 199; Justin Martyr, 199; his Apologies, 204—206, cf. 187; misappreciation of Antoninus Pius's attitude, 200; hatred of Jews towards Christians, 201; attitude of educated classes, 201—206; Lucian, 201, 202; Apuleius, 203; Aristides, 203; Celsus, 203; Crescens, 206; outlook for Christianity, 206.

Chronology of 140—143 A.D., difficulties in, 50, 51.

Claudius Severus, 125.

Clemens, C. Pactumius, *consul*, 113.

— Flavius, put to death under Domitian, 162—166.

— T. Varius, *praef. cohorti*, 71.

Coins as historical authority, 3, 6.

Collegia, synagogues exempted from law against, 152; suppressed in Bithynia-Pontus by Trajan, 167.

Comama damaged by earthquake, 47.

Commodus, L. Ceionius, *vide* Verus.

Consilium principis, origin of, 108, 109; two-fold developement, 109 reorganized by Hadrian especially for legal work, 110, 112; its constitution and activity under Hadrian, 17, 111; used for administrative, legislative and judicial work by Antoninus Pius, 112—114; *praef. praet.* admitted, 113; the jurisconsults employed by Antoninus Pius, 113; enactments of Antoninus Pius, 114.

Corcyra, Antoninus Pius's generosity to, 127.

INDEX.

Cornelius Victorinus, *praef. praet.*, 113.
Coronea in dispute with Thisbe, 129.
Costobocae, invasion of Greece by, 87.
Crescens, attacks of, on Justin Martyr, 205, 206.
Criobolia, 147.
Cyanese damaged by earthquake, 47.

Dacia, outbreak in, 82—85; date of disturbance, 82—84; reorganization of province, 83, 84; M. Statius Priscus governor, 83, 85; effects of reorganization, 87, 88.
Delphi, Antoninus Pius's generosity to, 127.
Decennial vows, 61, 62, 83, 88, 89; their origin, 62, 63.
Decentralization, results of, 120.
Diavolenus, *vide* Iavolenus.
Dinarchus, 73, 75.
Domitian, Jews and Christians under, 161—166.
Domitilla, Flavia, banished by Domitian, 162—166.

Earthquakes in Asia Minor under Antoninus Pius in two distinct circles, 46.
  i, *First*, 45 sqq.; Rhodes and S.W. Asia Minor suffer, 46; restoration of damage, 47, 48; Rhodes never recovers, 48.
  ii, *Second*, 67 sqq.; date, 68; W. and N.W. Asia Minor suffer, 68; restoration of damage, 68.
Eastern frontier, troubles on, 51, 74—81.

Eastern religions, 147, 148, 151; regulated by police, 151, 160, 161, 165, 193.
Egypt, revolt in, 73; date of revolt, 73, 74; its character, 75; suppressed by Antoninus Pius in person, 75, 76; buildings of the Emperor in the district, 76.
Epidaurus, buildings erected at, 56, 127, 144.
Etruscus, Valerius, 71.
Eusebius as historical authority, 5.
Eutropius as historical authority, 4.

Fabius Repentinus, *praef. praet.*, 113.
Faustina, Annia Galeria, married to Antoninus Pius, 13; received title of Augusta, 28; death, 48; character, 48, 49, 50; affection of Emperor for her, 49, 50; public honours in her lifetime, 49, 50; canonization, 50.
— Galeria (Minor), 14; marriage arrangements, 20, 32, 53, 58, 59, 99, 100; Augusta, 60.
Faustinianae, puellae, 121.
Favorinus, 68, 139.
Firmum Picenum, restoration of amphitheatre of, 116.
Flagitia cohaerentia nomini, 158, 202.
Founding of Rome, 900th anniversary of, 60, 61, 142.
Freedmen kept in check, 106, 126, 128.
Fregellae, bridge built by Antoninus Pius at, 116.
Fronto, M. Cornelius, as historical

212   INDEX.

authority, 2; tutor to M. Aurelius, 138; pedantic style, 138, 139.

Gaul, South, Antoninus Pius's connection with, 8, 56; road making in, 55, 56.
Gavius Maximus, *praef. praet.*, 113.
Gellius, Aulus, as historical authority, 2; miscellaneous nature of his writings, 139; chronicler of small talk, 139.
German revolt, 52, 53.
Glabrio, Acilius, put to death under Domitian, 162—166.
Government of Antoninus Pius, character of, 64, 97.
Graecina, Pomponia, 156, 157.

Hadrian, the *consilium* under, 17, 110—112; burial of, 25; ratification of his *Acta*, 26; ill-will of Senate to, 26; canonization, 27; his provincial governors not superseded by Antoninus Pius, 32; his bequests carried out, 37, 38, 116; his temple, 57, 66, 89; results of his decentralizing policy, 120; his severity to Jews, 176, 201; rescript to Minucius Fundanus, 178, 179; supposed leaning towards Christianity, 181.
Hadrianales, 27.
Heliodorus, 45.
Helius (=L. Aelius Verus), 18, 19.
Herodes Atticus, 17, 68, 144, 145.
Homullus, 95.
Hyginus, bishop of Rome, 191.

Iavolenus Priscus, jurisconsult, etc., 113.
Imperator, title of, 40, 44.
Imperial cult not specially supported by Antoninus Pius, 148, 149, 190; inherent limitations of this cult, 149.
Imperial families, similarity of names between, no proof of common stock, 19.
Imperial post, 126, 127.
Inscriptions as historical authority, 3, 6.
Ionia laid waste by earthquake, 68.
Isis, failure of attempts to expel the worship of, 148, 151.
Italy, welcome of Antoninus Pius by, 31; government restored to Senate, 115; *Aurum Coronarium* returned to the Italians, 115; buildings of Antoninus Pius in Italy, 116; gratitude of Italians, 116; other benefits to Italian towns, 116, 117; admission of Carni and Catuli to *Latinitas* at Tergeste, 117; burdens of municipal office, 118; *Ordo Augustalium*, 118, 119; generosity of private individuals heavily taxed, 119; bad results, 119, 120; results of Hadrian's decentralizing tendencies, 120.

Charitable endowments for boys and girls (*alimentariae*), 120—122; origin of these endowments, 120; Trajan's schemes, 120, 121; wide-spread organization of *pecunia alimentaria*, 121, 122; benefit to agriculture, 122.
Iulianus, P. Salvius, jurisconsult, etc., 113.

INDEX. 213

Ius Quintae Relationis granted to M. Aurelius, 59, 60, 100.

Jews, outbreak of the, under Antoninus Pius, 78; a theocracy, 152; tolerated in the Republic, 152; granted exemption by Augustus from objectionable duties, 152; synagogues not *collegia*, 152; western Jews more severely treated, 152, 153; national existence annihilated in 71 A.D., 153; subsequent position, 153; unpopularity, 153; fashionable craze of adopting Jewish customs leads to persecution under Domitian, 162; revolt under Barchochebas, 175; severity of Hadrian to the Jews, 176, 201; consequent hatred of Jews to Christians, 201.

Judaea, outbreak in, 78.

Jurisconsults in this reign, 112—114.

Justin Martyr as historical authority, 3, 187; strong personality, 199; his Apologies, 204—206; attacked by Crescens, 205, 206.

Ladii, the, 79.

Lambaesis, public works of Antoninus Pius at, 128.

Lanuvium, temples built by Antoninus Pius at, 117.

Latinitas conferred on Carni and Catuli, 117.

Laurentum, privileges granted by Antoninus Pius to, 117.

Lazai, the, *vide* Ladii.

Legislation of Antoninus Pius, 114.

Liberalitas bestowed by Antoninus Pius on nine occasions:—i, 37; ii, 53; iii, 53, 59; iv, 57, 59; v, 59, 63; vi, 66; vii, 76; viii, 88; ix, 90.

Literature of the period, poverty of, 130, 131;
 Lucian's satirical writings, 131—133; attacks on Christianity, 132, 133, 201, 202;
 Apuleius, 133—135, 203;
 Aristides' exaggeration, 3, 136; academic style, 135, 136; compared to Demosthenes, 136;
 M. Aurelius, 136—138; Eclectic and Stoic characteristics, 136, 137; not for publication, 137; good sentiments but small literary merit, 137, 138;
 M. Corn. Fronto, tutor to M. Aurelius, 138; pedantic style, 138, 139;
 A. Gellius, miscellaneous and trivial, 139;
 General triviality, 140.

Lorium, home of Antoninus Pius, 9, 90, 91.

Lucian as historical authority, 2; character of his writings, 131; satirical attacks, 131—133; attacks on Christianity, 132, 133, 201, 202; he indirectly advances Christianity, 133.

Lucilla, daughter of M. Aurelius, 59; married to L. Verus, 99.

Ludi circenses, theatre, etc. supported by Antoninus Pius, 29, 30, 50, 63, 66, 94, 116.

Maecianus, L. Volusius, jurisconsult, etc., 113.
Magna Mater, worship of, 147, 151.
Maiestas, Christians charged under head of, 162—165, 180, 186, 187, 191.
Malala as historical authority, 5.
Marcellus, L. Ulpius, jurisconsult, etc., 113.
Marcion, heresy of, 191.
Marius Maximus, 4.
Minucius, Fundanus, rescript of Hadrian to, 178, 179.
Mithras, worship of, 147, 148.
Molitor rerum novarum, Christian prisoner charged as, 162—164.
Mythological coins, 61, 95, 142—145.
Mythological worship encouraged by Antoninus Pius, 61, 94, 95, 117, 141—147, 190; a natural consequence of his temperament, 142; Hercules, etc., 142—145; Aeneas, etc., 143; Aesculapius, 127, 143, 144; temples, etc. built in Greece by Herodes Atticus, 144, 145; efforts for this reaction doomed to failure, 147, 151.

Narbo, Antoninus Pius builds baths and colonnade at, 128.
Nero, Christians persecuted under, 157—160.
Nomen ipsum of Christianity, 158—160, 166, 171, 172, 174, 178, 186, 192.
North-eastern frontier, troubles on, 51, 78, 79, 82—88.
Northern frontier, troubles on, 52, 53; road-making, 53.

Nullas expeditiones obiit, examination of this statement, 74—80.

Obstinatio of Christianity, 158, 169, 186.
Odium humani generis, 155—160; identification of Christianity with, 158, 159.
Olbia, 86.
Orosius as historical authority, 5.
Ostia, baths built by Antoninus Pius at, 38, 116; inscription in honour of the Emperor, 116.

Pallantium, a free town, 61.
Parthia, policy of preceding Emperors towards, 76, 77; relations of Antoninus Pius with, 77.
Patara damaged by earthquake, 47.
Pater Patriae, title of, 30, 38.
Pausanias as historical authority, 5.
Pius, bishop of Rome, 191, 199.
Plataea, *vide* Thebes.
Plinius Secundus, C., charitable endowments of, 120; dealings with Christians in Bithynia-Pontus, 166—174.
Polemon, 17, 68, 139.
Police regulation of foreign worships, 151, 160, 161, 165, 193.
Polycarp, martyrdom of, 193—199.
Pontifex Maximus, office of, reserved for the Emperor, 28.
Porolissum, Antoninus Pius restores Amphitheatre of, 127, 128.
Praefectus alimentorum, 122.
Praefectus praetorio admitted to the *consilium*, 113.
Praesens, C. Bruttius, 32.
Prastina, Messalinus, 70.

Priscianus, 107.
Priscus, M. Statius, governor of Dacia, 83, 85.
Proconsulare Imperium bestowed on M. Aurelius, 59, 100.
Proculus, C. Corn., 47.
Procuratores kept in check, 126.
Provinces, welcome of Antoninus Pius by, 30, 31; Hadrian's governors not superseded, 32; prudent policy of Emperors, 122, 123; prosperity of provinces, 123—125, 129; influence of Antoninus Pius with border-kings, 123; commercial facilities and security of travel, 124; care of the Emperor for the provinces, 125, 126; provincial governors for long periods, 126; *Aurum coronarium* partly returned, 126; *procuratores* kept well in check, 126; abuses of Imperial post removed, 126, 127; Antoninus Pius refuses to go on tours, 127; his generosity to the provinces, 127, 128; accessibility to provincials, 128; attention to detail, 129, 130.
Ptolemaeus and Lucius, martyrdom of, 191—193.
Puteoli, sea-wall built by the Emperor, 38, 116; founding of games, 116.

Quadi, King appointed over, 51; doubtful allegiance, 51, 52.
Quadratus (Apologist), 176—178; value of evidence of Apologists, 187.
Quadratus, L. Statius, *procos. Asiae*, 193, 194, 198.

Quaestor pecuniae alimentariae, 121.
Quattuor viri consulares, 15, 104, 105, 115.

Religio licita, 153, 160.
Religion, a political affair under the Roman government, 150; theoretically strange worship is treason, 150; modifications owing to conquest, 150; incorporation of new gods, 151; universal toleration except for dangerous creeds, 151.
Rhodes damaged by earthquake, 46.
Road-making in Antoninus Pius's reign, 53—55, 116.
Rome, welcome of Antoninus Pius by, 31.

Saltus Aurasius, 70.
Sarapis, worship of, 148.
Sarmatae, the, 86.
Scriptores Historiae Augustae as historical authority, 3, 4; based on Marius Maximus, 4.
Scylacium, water-supply furnished by Antoninus Pius, 116.
Senate well treated by Antoninus Pius, 27—30, 95, 104, 105; leanings of Antoninus Pius towards, 103; its weakness recognized, 104; presents from the Emperor to individual senators, 104; unwillingness to canonize Hadrian, 104; government of Italy restored to, 105; no senator put to death by Antoninus Pius, 106; goodwill towards Antoninus Pius,

106, 107; honours willingly paid to the Imperial family, 108.

Senex, Iulius, 69.

Signia, public works of Antoninus Pius at, 38.

Smyrna, 129; Christian persecution in, 193—199.

Stratonicea damaged by earthquake, 47.

Syria, visit of Antoninus Pius and M. Aurelius to, 74—80; buildings erected by the Emperor in the district, 81.

Tarracina, harbour restored by Antoninus Pius at, 116.

Tatius Maximus, *praef. praet.*, 113.

Taurobolia, 147.

Tauroscythae, the, 86.

Telesphorus, martyrdom of, 190, 191.

Tergeste, admission of Carni and Catuli to *Latinitas* in, 117.

Thebes in dispute with Plataea, 129.

Thespiae, Antoninus Pius's generosity to, 127.

Thisbe, *vide* Coronea.

Titianus, Atilius, 107.

Torquatus, C. Bellicius, *consul*, 113.

Torture in Christian trials, 186.

Tribunicia Potestas, when renewed by Antoninus Pius, 33, 34, 90; not numbered on coins of Antoninus Pius till 148 A.D., 87; bestowed on M. Aurelius, 58, 59, 100.

Urbicus, Q. Lollius, governor of Britain, 42, 43; *praef. urbi*, 191, 192.

Valens, L. Fulvius Aburnius, jurisconsult, etc., 113.

Valentinus, heresy of, 191.

Verecundia, aqueduct of Antoninus Pius at, 128.

Verus, L. Aelius, *vide* Helius.

— L. Ceionius Commodus, son of Helius, 18; adopted by Antoninus Pius, 20, 98; marriage arrangements upset, 20, 32, 99; early life and education, 57, 102; marriage, 102; honours, 102, 103; no favourite with Antoninus Pius, 102, 103.

— Vindius, jurisconsult, etc., 113.

Victor, S. Aurelius, as historical authority, 5.

Vologeses, King of Parthia, 80, 81.

Xiphilinus as historical authority, 5, 6.

Zonaras as historical authority, 5, 6.